CAMBRIDGE STUDIES IN PHILOSOPHY

Analyzing Love

CAMBRIDGE STUDIES IN PHILOSOPHY

General editor SYDNEY SHOEMAKER

Advisory editors J.E.J. ALTHAM, SIMON BLACKBURN,
GILBERT HARMAN, MARTIN HOLLIS, FRANK JACKSON,
JONATHAN LEAR, JOHN PERRY, BARRY STROUD

Analyzing Love

Robert Brown

The right of the
University of Cambridge
to print and publish
all kinds of books
was granted by law
in 1534.
The University has printed
and published continuously
since 1584.

Cambridge University Press

Cambridge
New York   New Rochelle
Melbourne   Sydney

Published by the Press Syndicate of the University of Cambridge
The Pitt Building, Trumpington Street, Cambridge CB2 1RP
32 East 57th Street, New York, NY 10022, USA
10 Stamford Road, Oakleigh, Melbourne 3166, Australia

© Cambridge University Press 1987

First published 1987
Reprinted 1989

Printed in the United States of America

Library of Congress Cataloging-in-Publication Data
Brown, Robert, 1920–
Analyzing love.
(Cambridge studies in philosophy)
1. Love. I. Title. II. Series.
BD436.B76 1987   128′.3   87–9342

British Library Cataloguing in Publication Data
Brown, Robert
Analyzing love.—(Cambridge studies
in philosophy).
1. Love
I. Title
128′.3   BD436

ISBN 0 521 34038 1

Contents

v

Preface

This book was intended to be, and remains, a short introduction to a subject whose boundaries recede with each attempt to characterize them. Nevertheless, the role of benevolence, care, solicitude, and love in human life is so obvious and important that at first glance any new discussion of it may seem to be redundant. Yet the truth is otherwise. For the character of personal relations in advanced industrial societies is constantly being altered by the ceaseless changes in the social institutions of which those relations are a part. Hence as members of such societies, it is natural for us to wish to examine those relationships over a period of time in order to understand what sort of people we are in the process of becoming. Before we can do that, however, we have to try to remind ourselves of the nature of the emotions and attitudes that are embedded in some of our ways of dealing with other people, and with animals and objects. Love and care are basic elements in many of these practices, and thus the former will attract attention whenever the latter are under close scrutiny. For this and other reasons there has been renewed interest in recent years concerning the connections among the different emotions and various traits of human character on the one hand, and the links between both of these and the moral virtues and vices on the other. In *Analyzing Love* I have attempted to discuss at length only some aspects of one emotion, but it should be clear that a powerful motive for doing so is eventually to shed light, if possible, on our judgments – or misjudgments – of human character.

The scope and complexity of these interrelated problems is revealed by the extended treatment given to them in Roger Scruton's recent book *Sexual Desire*. He explores what he takes to be the psychological and moral implications of the view that in normal sexual desire the partners desire each other as self-conscious, free, and responsible moral agents whose state of arousal is cooperative and reciprocal. The discussion of these implications leads Scruton to take up a great range of topics in addition to sexual desire: Among them are the first-person perspective, intentionality, moral theory, the concept of a person, religion and sex, and of course love. In *Analyzing Love* I consider only a few of these. This text was completed before Scruton's book reached me, and while some of our conclusions are similar, they are reached by independent routes that, if pursued further, would diverge toward disparate outcomes. I have resisted the strong temptation to alter my text in order to take account of the many important, interesting, and also highly contentious, points that are put forward in *Sexual Desire*, especially since they do not affect my comments on Scruton's earlier views. To succumb to the temptation would have been to write a very different, and much longer, book.

For aid in what I have written I am particularly indebted to John Passmore for his detailed and helpful comments on an earlier draft. I also thank Ann Lane for her perceptive criticism of certain sections. Vibeke Wetselaar and Wendie Woods have shared the burden of typing the manuscript. I am grateful not only for their willingness to take on the task but also for the competence with which it was done.

Introduction: The problems

We seem to possess all the information that we could possibly wish to have concerning love as a relationship between people; and yet some apparently simple questions on the topic have received rather different answers; and in some cases no clear answer at all. If A loves B, must A, as a matter of definition, want to benefit and cherish B, wish to keep company and communicate with B, and have B reciprocate this beneficial interest? 'Yes', says Gabrielle Taylor, for 'we view love as a give-and-take relationship, so the essential wants will have to reflect this feature'. (1976, p. 154) 'No', remarks J.F.M. Hunter, 'some are able to love without their love being reciprocated while others can only love those who love them'. (1983, p. 70) Curiously enough, however, Hunter does not mention the fact that the former might wish their love to be reciprocated. David Hamlyn agrees that reciprocity is not required and suggests that neither is the wish for association and communication. 'Suppose', he writes, 'that someone has got to the point of recognizing the absolutely disastrous character of a relationship. It is possible for them to renounce it and any desire for its continuance while still loving the person concerned'. (1978, p. 13)

Again, we can ask whether A must love B – or usually loves B – for what A takes to be worthwhile qualities or features. More generally, we can ask whether anyone ever loves another person simply because he or she values certain qualities of the beloved. We can also ask, as Taylor does, whether love and infatuation are distinguished by the presence of such valuation in the former case and its absence in

1

the latter case – whether the infatuated person simply desires the loved one independently of any evaluation by the agent of the qualities of the beloved. If this distinction holds, then Hamlyn must be mistaken in claiming that 'loving someone or something is not incompatible with having no respect for them, finding them in many ways distasteful, or recognizing in them a whole series of bad qualities which are not over-ridden by good qualities'. (p. 13)

To Donne's question, 'Now thou hast lov'd me one whole day, To morrow when thou leav'st, what wilt thou say?' many answers have been given. It is a commonplace to distinguish, as Alan Goldman does, between sexual desire and 'love as a long-term, deep emotional relationship between two individuals . . . permanent, at least in intent, and more or less exclusive'. (1976, p. 273) There is 'fleeting sexual desire', but not, in his usage of the term 'love', fleeting or casual love. (p. 273) On the other side there is Roger Trigg's view 'that one could have a momentary feeling of love or hope if the context is specific enough, and if there is an explanation why the emotion is only momentary'. For if we claim that momentary feelings of this sort cannot be emotions, 'we have to ask how long we have to experience an emotion before we recognize it as one'. The answer, he thinks, is that we do not have to 'wait five minutes to see if we still view a situation as threatening before claiming that we are afraid'. (1970, pp. 43–4) This answer is not, apparently, one which Taylor would think applicable to love. She writes:

Unlike other emotions, love is not 'occasional': while it is appropriate to speak of an occasion for being angry, afraid, grateful etc., we can hardly talk in this way of love. This is partly so because to link love with particular occasions would leave open the possibility of its being very short-lived indeed, and this we are not prepared to do'. (1976, p. 161)

But should love properly be classified as an emotion? Taylor seems to think that love is a complex and unusual emotion.

(pp. 161–4) Ronald De Sousa, on the other hand, suggests that because love is so complex, incorporating as it does 'whole complexes of particular feelings, expectations, long term patterns of intercourse and social sanctions', it should not, perhaps, be thought of as an emotion. (1980, p. 291) This same view would, presumably, tell against the existence of short-term love. Or is the situation that there are momentary feelings of love that, though lacking these long-term patterns and complexes, are still genuine emotions? The answer is not established. However, if love, at least in some of its forms, is not an ordinary emotion, what are we to call it? 'The emotions', says Aristotle in the *Rhetoric*, 'are all those feelings that so change men as to affect their judgements, and that are also attended by pain or pleasure'. (1984, 1378a 20–1, p. 2195) According to Roger Scruton, love is in fact more like an emotion than like an attitude. For love, like most of the other emotions, has particular things or people as its objects whereas attitudes 'are directed towards things as tokens or instantiations of some type or property'. (1971, p. 41) Attitudes, Scruton believes, can be further distinguished from emotions by the fact that in the former 'the elements of belief and intention' are dominant whereas in emotions they are not. In emotions, 'desires and wishes tend to exist in the context of relatively few beliefs and of perhaps no definite intentions'. (p. 30) Love, apparently, belongs in this context.

One further question that has been much discussed, and is worth considering here, is whether love occupies some sort of special position among the emotions – if it is an emotion. It is sometimes suggested, for instance, that love is unusual among the emotions because there are so few constraints on what can be loved. Yet what, then, about fear? We can be afraid of almost anything; yet fear is the very model of an ordinary and basic emotion. On the other hand, it is sometimes claimed that love and fear differ radically in that we can usually, although not always, give reasons why we fear someone or something but often find it impossible to give reasons for loving whatever we love. Is it, then, that the possible objects of our love are so various simply because there are explanatory, or causal, reasons for our loving whatever we love, but there are – and can be – no justificatory reasons for our loves? Perhaps, for example, to love a woman is to be attracted to her as someone whom we evaluate as being worthwhile in herself, and hence as someone for whom we can offer no further or additional reason for loving. If so, does this set love off from the other emotions? Is the concept of love, just because love requires no justification, more resistant to analysis than such other common emotions as fear, anger, joy, grief, and envy?

Yet, to put forward such questions as these does not at once indicate why they are worth pursuing. What more general purposes do they serve – what more general benefits do they confer on us? Why, after all, should we treat them as worthy of more than after-dinner conversation? The answer is that there are at least three good reasons for discussing these questions, reasons that apply both to the emotions in general and to love in particular.

The simplest reason is that because the emotions of love and affection occupy such a large part of our lives, we spend a great deal more time acting under the influence of these emotions than we do in considering their character. In consequence, we have in use a large array of concepts that are more often employed than examined. The vocabulary by which we express or describe love and affection is known to almost everyone: Terms of endearment are learned at an early age. But the logical relationships that hold among the terms of affection – the inferences that can properly be drawn from the speech acts that incorporate these terms – are known to only a proportion of those who use the vocabulary. The same holds true of anger, hate, and the other emotions. So to guard against basic disagreements of the sort that we have been instancing, we need, at the very least, to scrutinize the terms in which they, and hence the questions that produce such disagreements, are phrased.

The second reason is that, as Errol Bedford put it,

emotion words form part of the vocabulary of appraisal and criticism, and a number of them belong to the more specific language of moral criticism. Normally, the verbs in their first-person use imply the speaker's assessment of something, and in their third-person use they carry an implication about an assessment by the person they refer to. (1957, p. 214)

Thus the emotion-terms 'irascible', 'jealous', and 'infatuated' are commonly used to condemn; others such as 'affectionate', 'loving', and 'benevolent' are ordinarily terms of approval. Moreover, as Bedford goes on to show, some emotion-words such as 'contempt', 'disgust', 'pride', 'regret', 'remorse', and 'shame' presuppose certain moral assessments. We cannot, for example, feel remorse for an action that we assess as completely evil. Some emotion-words cannot be used appropriately unless such judgments and appraisals have already been made and can be assumed to exist. Hence if we are to understand the relationships between these evaluations and our feelings – between our critical judgments and the statements of our emotions – we have to consider how questions of appropriateness, rationality, and justification can arise in connection with the feeling of emotions. Once we do consider the problem of how we criticize or justify our feeling, or our displaying, at a given time, a particular emotion such as love, it becomes obvious that we must deal with the disagreements with which we began. For they spring, in part, from differences of view, and in some cases confusion, concerning, first, the nature of the assessments and judgments that are commonly embedded in our various uses of emotion-terms and, second, the relationship in general between assessments and judgments (or beliefs) on the one hand and emotions on the other.

That assessments, judgments, and emotional agitation can

all three vary in at least partial independence of each other is quite clear. Our emotional fear of someone can linger on long after our original judgment of that person as a threat to us has been given up. We identify it as fear rather than hatred or disgust because we recall its original source. Similarly, a woman's love for her husband can change into dislike even though her appraisal of his character or personality is unaltered. She can simply become bored with him for displaying the same familiar characteristics, each of which she still values but no longer wishes to observe at such close quarters. Her sensations, feelings, and desires concerned with him have altered although her beliefs about him, and her evaluations of him have not: The youthful innocence, for example, that once compelled her affection no longer does because other aspects of the situation have changed for her. However, while evaluations, beliefs, desires, and emotional agitation (feelings, sensations, physiological effects) are all different from each other, we shall see that it does not follow from this fact – and indeed is not true – that the various emotional states such as hatred, fear, anger, jealousy, and love can be identified and distinguished in the absence of the characteristic evaluations and judgments that help to constitute them. If we know only that a person is undergoing heart palpitations, has an upset stomach, clammy skin, muscular weakness, and a desire to rest, we cannot even conclude that the person is in an emotional state rather than merely being physiologically disturbed. We certainly cannot discover which emotion the person is undergoing even when we learn that he or she received a telephone call and that the physiological symptoms followed soon after. We do not know whether the person is almost prostrate with grief or weak with joy, afraid of the worst or giddy with hope.

To this it is sometimes replied that our knowledge of the agent's assessments and judgments in the situation may not help much. For the agent may feel pride when his own judgments of his situation should have led him to feel regret, or may feel shame when he should have felt only embarrassment. His judgments did not produce in him the sensations, feelings, and desires that fitted his circumstance. The wrong emotion was present; the agent's beliefs about his situation and his evaluation of it did not lead him to feel the appropriate emotion.

A brief, but nevertheless correct, answer to this objection is this: How does the agent know which emotional state he was in when he claimed to have felt pride rather than regret, embarrassment rather than shame? Often he knows before he has had the opportunity to observe his own behaviour or has performed any action. He had an unfulfillable wish to disappear instantly from the scene of his embarrassment or feels the futile desire to undo what he has done. He hopes that the situation in which he finds himself will be short-lived and that his friends will not learn of it. He cannot see how to rebut the complaint laid against him, how to make his innocence plausible, how to repair the damage he has done. But when he knows what emotion he is experiencing he usually, although not always, knows this because he is aware of what it is in his situation that has produced his emotion, and thus what would have to be changed for it to disappear. The inadvertently offensive remark he has just made to his friend would have to remain unsaid; the disfigurement of his face would have to be concealed; the public honours now being bestowed on him would have to be withdrawn. With these changes his embarrassment, his shame, and his pride would vanish.

Yet a person knows what has produced his emotion in such cases only because he has judged and evaluated some feature of his situation as being of a certain type – for example, as being socially awkward for him and hence embarrassing; or as being the public exposure of a misdeed that he wished to keep secret from those who respect him, but will now make him feel shame. Without these judgments and evaluations he would not know why he was agitated, or what connection

7

his desires and wishes had with his situation, for the same desires and wishes can appear in different emotions: The desire to run away is common in both fear and shame, and the wish to benefit someone is present in both love and pity. Therefore, given the agent's own judgments and evaluation, it is a mistake to think that a person can experience an emotion inappropriate to the person's own assessment of the circumstances. A person cannot judge and evaluate an action as being a shameful one for him or her to have done, and then feel nothing, or feel some quite different emotion such as anger. To assess and evaluate one's situation as being shameful or fearful or disgusting or pitiable is at the same time, and thereby, to feel shame or fear or disgust or self-pity. If this were not so, then a person could claim, due to his or her situation, to be in a state of shame or fear or disgust or pity while feeling none of these emotions. But in that case all that the agent would be claiming would be that he or she was in a state worthy of those particular emotions, or in a state to which these emotions were appropriate. The agent would be claiming to be only a critical spectator of the situation and not a participant in it.

Of course an agent can misjudge the situation – assume blame where none exists – or undervalue some element of the situation so that the agent can feel the 'wrong' or inappropriate emotion. A woman can feel shame when she mistakenly blames herself for something beyond her control, or can take pride in a deed that a morally less primitive person would have regretted. However, to do this is not to feel an emotion inappropriate to one's own assessment and judgment of a situation. It is to make judgments and evaluations that are inappropriate to the actual situation. But the emotion felt is entirely appropriate to the agent's own assessment of her circumstances and could not have arisen without it. There is an important, though sometimes neglected, difference between someone judging that she is in a situation in which she should, but does not, feel shame or fear, and someone judging

8

that her situation is indeed a shameful or fearful one. Assessments of the latter sort are recognitions of the kind of emotion being felt by the agent; those of the former sort are agreements to forms or standards of behaviour that the agent is not in fact observing or carrying out, and in consequence of this, represent an acceptance of the propriety of certain emotions that the agent is not in fact feeling.

It is a more general point that the term 'emotion' is used ambiguously to refer either to physical and mental agitation of specifiable kinds or to these agitations when they are produced by specifiable types of judgments and evaluations. It is possible for someone to be in a state of emotional agitation simply as a result of illness or electrical stimulation of the brain, and thus to be in an emotional state without undergoing any specific emotion such as jealousy or rage. The converse is obviously not possible. When people speak of someone feeling the emotion appropriate to his or her situation, they are referring to specific emotions. Hence they are referring not only to the agent's agitation but to specific types of judgments, evaluations, and desires that he or she should have and did exhibit. But when it is suggested that emotion is unnecessary in human life and is a primitive feature of human behaviour, reference is being made only to the mental and physical agitation that appears in every specific emotion and not to its associated judgments and assessments. If this suggestion were realized, the appraisal of a situation as dangerous or hateful would remain, and so would the impulse to retreat or retaliate, but the accompanying physiological effects would be absent. It is this ambiguous use of the term 'emotion' that encourages the view that since judgments and emotional agitation are clearly different, the former play little part in our recognition and experience of the various emotions. This is not true, for while without specific sorts of judgments and assessments we might undergo a general emotional agitation, it could not amount to any specific emotion. The agitation would and could not be anger, hate, envy, joy, or any other of the distinctive and individual emotional states we now recognize.

In the case of love, all these considerations concerning judgment and emotion have important consequences. For the presence of love is commonly taken to be a necessary condition of the existence of human society. Freud expresses a common opinion when he says that 'in the development of mankind as a whole, just as in individuals, love alone acts as the civilizing factor in the sense that it brings a change from egoism to altruism'. (1953, p. 103) The narcissism that is revealed, he says, in the wide-spread human antipathy to strangers is absent within an established group. Its members, he writes,

tolerate the peculiarities of its other members, equate themselves with them, and have no feeling of aversion towards them. Such a limitation of narcissism can, according to our theoretical views, only be produced by one factor, a libidinal tie with other people. Love for oneself knows only one barrier – love for others, love for objects. (p. 102)

If this claim is correct, then it is important for us to be clear as to the character of those attachments and the judgments of value to which they give rise. If Freud's claim about the libidinal tie within groups is incorrect, then it is equally important that we distinguish clearly between the emotions that maintain groups and the love that binds together individual members of such groups. For the different emotions in the two cases will require different forms of critical appraisal and justification.

The third reason for trying to answer our earlier questions is that they bear on the problem of how, and to what extent, reason can cause or control or eliminate an emotion. Not only do changes in our information often produce changes in our emotions – so that, for example, we may no longer be afraid of a noise that we learn is made by our harmless cat – but our capacity to understand, although not perhaps to feel, any particular emotion requires us to possess the concepts that the emotion either incorporates or presupposes. While as infants we can feel fear without possessing the concept of fear, we cannot know or understand that we feel fear unless we also possess the concept of danger, harm, or threat; and we cannot know that we feel shame unless we already possess the concept of blameworthiness; nor can we know that we feel remorse without having the concept of guilt. It follows from the presence of these relationships that as our concepts increase in variety, scope, and depth, so also do the emotions that depend upon and embody those concepts. When our notions of guilt are deepened and extended, they similarly affect the emotion of guilt that we feel and the feelings of remorse that are produced by that emotion. All these connections remain hidden from us unless we are clear as to the way in which emotion-terms are actually used to explain our behaviour. They do so, it is generally agreed, not merely by being used to report our inward experiences – our sensations and feelings – but by referring also to our beliefs, desires, appraisals, and evaluations. In performing this task, our use of emotion-words presupposes both a system of social interactions and an interplay between our evaluative judgments and the desires that move us to action. Therefore, explanations of behaviour in terms of emotions reveal much about the role of reason in human actions. But this role is most clearly revealed when we examine specific cases – as we are proposing to do in the case of love. We cannot hope to answer, in this way, the triad of large questions that we have listed. But we can reasonably hope to show why the effort to do so should continue.

We can best do this, perhaps, by noting the kinds of specific questions that arise within the topic of love, for it is with some of these narrower questions that we shall be concerned. There is, first, the problem of identifying the relevant features of love: its distinction from liking and benevolence, on the one hand, and from sexual desire on the other; the kinds of objects that can be loved and the kinds of judgments and

11

objectives required by it. There is, second, the problem of recognizing love, both in its inception and its maintenance, and hence the grounds for claiming it to be present or absent in particular cases. Whereas the first problem is that of what constitutes love, the second problem is that of our ability to identify its presence. The third problem, then, is twofold: It is that of comparing love with common emotions such as fear and anger; but it is also that of contrasting emotions generally with attitudes, and of finding an appropriate place for love with respect to these categories. Finally, we have to deal with the problem, if there is one, of justifying our loves, of deciding whether we can have, or need, reasons for loving, what sorts of judgments are displayed in love, and what grounds we can have for criticizing the judgments and evaluations made by lovers of the objects of their love.

We shall take up these problems roughly in the order just given, although Chapter 1 surveys and briefly touches upon a number of issues that are either dealt with more fully later or reappear in a different setting – love as a nonpractical relationship, for example, or love as a judgment of inherent worth. But embedded in these various problems and issues are two questions of special interest and importance, both worth more attention than can be given to them here. Each applies both to objects and people, but in some respects their application to people raises more interesting issues than does their application to objects. One question is 'What exactly is it that the lover cherishes?' The other question is 'On what grounds can someone's love be criticized?' These questions are important, in part, because they direct us to the evaluations that people make of each other's character and personality taken as a whole rather than to the various qualities and attributes displayed in it. Since total, or comprehensive, evaluations of a person's character and personality are often made by friends and enemies in addition to lovers, it is reasonable to ask how the judgments of the latter group differ, in their justification, from those of the two former groups. To ask this question is thus to raise the question how one can defend or criticize such judgments, not only those made by oneself but those made by other people. It is also to ask under what conditions agreement on any given evaluation is possible.

Sadly, in recent years not as much philosophical attention has been paid to such total evaluations of character and personality as the importance of the topic demands. For we make these evaluations almost every day in a wide variety of social situations, whether in obituaries or soap opera, in character assassination or letters of reference. In each case we are making judgments whose grounds may or may not be known to us. But the connection of these grounds with the character of the people being judged is often obscure – obscure not merely because of errors of fact but also because of uncertainty as to the value that ought to be attributed, in a given situation, to the actions and capacities as a whole of a particular person. The example of love is useful here because in loving someone we are making a total or comprehensive evaluation of the beloved under circumstances extremely familiar to us. We ought, therefore, by examining such evaluations to put ourselves in a position to cast some light on character evaluations in general. We shall not be able to extend our discussion as far as that in this study. But we can try here to make such discussion easier in the future, and our examination of love will have that as one of its aims.

1

Love and its objects

CONSTRAINTS ON LOVING

Love is commonly reckoned to be one emotion among many. But how many emotions we think there are depends on what account we adopt of the necessary and sufficient conditions for something to be an emotion. If we think that emotions are simply our awareness of the physiological changes produced in us by our perception of certain sorts of objects, then we can try to count the different sorts of objects that are capable of causing these bodily sensations in us: for example, frightening objects, extraordinary objects, delightful ones. Or we can try to count emotions by distinguishing the different patterns of these physiological changes that certain sorts of objects and situations produce in us: in sorrow, irregular heart beats combined with weeping and trembling, for instance. However, if the view adopted is the one that we shall employ here, an emotional state consists in abnormal bodily changes caused by the agent's evaluation or appraisal of some object or situation that the agent believes to be of concern to him or her. Distinguishing such states from each other, and hence counting them, will require us to distinguish the different kinds of evaluations and appraisals embedded in them – evaluations, for example, of situations as being inexplicably strange or embarrassing or pathetic or pitiful or appealing. Since not all societies make these same sorts of evaluations, some emotions named and recognized in one society can be nameless and unfamiliar in another. Thus the German *Schadenfreude*, or malicious glee, is a response that is familiar outside Germany but perhaps not common enough

14

in some societies for it to be classified by their members as an ordinary emotion.

The various emotions, whether named or nameless, are often referred to as complex patterns of attention that are directed at specifiable classes of objects. These patterns consist in thoughts, desires, physiological effects, feelings, and sensations. For love, this pattern may be of special complexity since, it is often pointed out, there appear to be fewer restrictions on what we can love than there are on the objects toward which we can direct our other emotions, such as anger, greed, shame, fear, chagrin, joy, pride, or delight. This is because, as has been said many times in the history of the topic, there is nothing in particular that we have to believe about the object of our love in order to make it a possible recipient of our affectionate and tender care – of our heart-felt attraction to it. That feeling-laden care is ours to give as freely as we please whatever the nature of its object and whether we think it can or cannot exist, whether we think it morally good or bad. It follows that love is not always a practical emotion in Aristotle's sense: That is, some forms of love are not always directed, as practical emotions are by definition, at a particular sort of goal that is pursued in a particular sort of way. Parental love of a child, for example, need be directed at only the most general of goals – that of the child's greatest good – and a parent's love may be expressed in a wide variety of ways over a long period of time.

In contrast is Aristotle's characterization of anger as a practical emotion, for it is, he says, 'a desire accompanied by pain for a conspicuous revenge for a conspicuous slight'. (1984, 1378^{b}1 31–2, A2195) Since revenge can only be obtained by specific sorts of action, anger must be a practical emotion. But this is surely a characterization not of anger in general but of one form of righteous anger or indignation, and this emotion is taken by Aristotle to be, like shame, a nonpractical emotion. Clearly, anger, rage, and fury are often present without a desire for revenge: We can be angry at someone's

15

foolhardiness without wishing the person harm, although we may wish the person to make reparation or at least to acknowledge wrongdoing. Yet even these desires may be absent; someone may have an uncontrollable outburst of anger at the pure misery of his situation – for instance, at the violence of the storm that has thrown him up on a God-forsaken shore. Thus anger in itself is a nonpractical emotion that can express mere frustration or be suffered in silence without any desire to pursue a specific action. Indignation, on the other hand, is a more practical emotion that embodies the view that someone has been treated unjustly, shamefully, or contemptibly (Fortenbaugh, 1975, pp. 79–83) by someone else who should make reparation.

We fear something only if we think it does or could exist and is bad for us, or can have bad consequences for those close to us. We are indignant only at states of affairs that are in our view wrongs whose agents should acknowledge as such. This is true even when the offence is one of omission: Someone can be indignant, for example, at the lack of fire protection that should have been given by those in authority. In hatred we wish to destroy or eliminate something whose existence for some reason – perhaps a moral one – offends us. But can we also hate what no longer exists? Can we hate Hitler's political actions, for example, or the thought that American Indians were once hunted down and shot as Sunday sport?

Clearly, we can feel love for something that we believe does not exist – our dead child, for instance. Feeling hate is closely similar, and thus both love and hate are different in this respect from fear. But they are less different from indignation. To say that I am indignant now because of some dead agent's misdeed is possible but somewhat inappropriate since the wrong done cannot be admitted or redressed by the person responsible. There is no agent to whom I can address my complaint.

There is no such inappropriateness in hating, or loving, something or someone. For in saying, 'I hated the very thought that she was prepared to divorce him', I am some-

16

times saying two things: that I disliked thinking that the divorce might take place and, of course, that I should have hated the event itself if it were to occur. These are two different objects of dislike since I can dislike the one without disliking the other. In hating this thought I wish the state of affairs to which the thought refers not to exist or not to have existed; but I also wish not to have to contemplate the possibility that the state of affairs has existed or might come to exist. The sense of 'hate' seems to be the same in both 'I hated the divorce' and 'I hated thinking that the divorce might actually take place'. In both cases I want the object of my dislike – the divorce and my thinking of the divorce – not to have existed, although once in existence its removal may be acknowledged by me to have become impossible.

In parallel fashion, to say that I love the thought of my marrying her is sometimes to say that I both cherish the prospect of doing so, and should cherish actually being married to her. I can, of course, cherish one of these without cherishing the other, and sometimes there is no such distinction to be drawn. Cherishing the prospect of marriage can be simply liking or enjoying the thought of being married rather than holding dear the thought itself. But when the very thought itself is treasured it is not merely liked; it is valued in its own right. People can become as fond of their own ideas as they can of many other sorts of things. Some of the behaviour possible and appropriate to each sort will differ, but the attachment is the same.

LIKING AND LOVING

Liking, or even loving, someone's company is different from liking or loving the companion, although our pleasure in the association is often accompanied by strong affection for our associate. Yet it is possible to enjoy greatly the wit, amiability, and sociability of a colleague without being warmly attached to him or her in other respects. We can like the

17

qualities, or the person's exemplification of those qualities, while not liking or having much interest in the remainder of the person's character and values. A drinking companion need not be welcome in more than that role. Similarly, we can develop and display great liking for a specific activity or animal – dressage riding and the Andalusian horse used to do it, for example – while having no inclination to devote our entire life to that kind of riding or to that particular horse. Our attachment in all such cases need not be calm and controlled, but nevertheless it is confined to identifiable periods of our daily routines. We need not, and often do not and cannot, generalize these attachments so that they become interwoven with our deepest hopes, wishes, and values. Despite this, we still speak of our affection, liking, and preference for such pursuits, or of our attachment and devotion to them – in brief, our love of them.

Now to this last use of the word 'love' it is often complained that there are important differences between liking and loving, that we can like, or be drawn and attracted to, animals, situations, activities, judgments, beliefs, and policies, but that we can love only people. So while we can like and appreciate, even cherish, our companion's wit and amiability, we cannot love these qualities; we can only love the person – if we do. However, the basis for this distinction does not lie in our actual usage of the terms 'like' and 'love.' English speakers, like French and German speakers, quite commonly assert that they love their dogs, their cars, their golf games, their swimming pools, their jobs, the view from the front veranda, and their native country. They treat their love of these things as simply a more developed form of liking them, and believe, presumably, that 'liking' and 'loving' overlap in sense. 'Avoir l'amour de quelque chose' can mean either 'having a liking for something' or 'having a love of something', and 'Les avions sont ses amours' says that 'He loves aircraft' or that 'Aircraft are his passion'. Similarly, in German *liebhaben* can mean either 'to like' or 'to love': Germans can also say, 'Ich liebe die blumen', if they like – or love – flowers. This overlap need not, of course, prevent us from agreeing that there are differences between some forms of liking and some sorts of love. But it does indicate that these differences, if they exist, are not revealed by the mere common application of the terms themselves; we have to begin by looking further at the distinctions drawn in common speech between different types of loving as against liking.

One familiar but important difference between liking and at least one sort of love is that the latter is a disposition to be subject to emotional episodes or states in which bodily changes, sensations, and feelings play an indispensable role. 'Liking', however, is not the name of an emotion, and hence not of a disposition to be subject to emotional states. Instead, it is variously a synonym for 'enjoying', 'wanting', 'preferring', or 'choosing', and while desires and preferences are common constituents of emotions, they are not in themselves states of emotion. To desire to have short sleeves, or to prefer them to long sleeves, is not in itself to be in an emotional state. Again, to like bushwalking is to enjoy or take pleasure in doing it, and we can express this by saying that we love bushwalking. But 'enjoyment' and 'pleasure' are not the names either of kinds of emotions, or of specific emotions, although some emotions such as love, awe, gratitude, and pride are often accompanied by pleasure and desires and some people enjoy being angry. 'She would like to have (desires to have) rice instead of potatoes' expresses a preference, and a customer who says, 'I like (desire) this one', and hands it to the shop assistant is both exercising a choice and expressing a preference. The customer need not, however, be displaying an emotion called 'liking' or 'desiring,' or indeed, be feeling any emotion whatsoever. Similarly, a woman who says to a man, 'I like you very much' may either be confessing to love or doing the opposite: emphasizing that while she takes pleasure in his company, and in that sense is attracted to him, and perhaps concerned for his well-being, she is not in love with

19

him and hence lacks strong feelings toward him. She is distinguishing between liking him, however much, and being in love with him. It is a further question whether she is also suggesting that while not in love with him, she cherishes or loves him as a friend.

Sometimes, however, it is objected that we can love only people and animals because our apparent love for other things is never genuine love. Richard Taylor, for example, has written:

> Loving an *object* is not really loving *it* at all; instead, it is an expression of self-love. A person who takes pride in his possessions, who glories in them, quite clearly does not love them for their own sake, but for his. They are just ornaments. A man's relationship to fine cars, buildings, or whatever, is exactly that of a woman's relationship to her jewelry. They are loved because they enhance their owners. (1982, p. 146)

In this passage Taylor is suggesting that the so-called love of objects is not genuine since they are not loved for their own sake. They are valued only insofar as they contribute to their owners' self-esteem. However it is not obvious why pride of possession is supposed to be the only form that love of objects takes. That many objects, and even some animals and people, are treated as 'just ornaments' is indisputable. That all objects for which we claim to have affection are loved because they satisfy their owners self-love is indisputably false. For we have no adequate reason to believe that loving an object must always be an expression of self-love – that self-love and its satisfaction motivate all our love of objects. This only appears to be so if we characterize the objects as things in whose possession we take pride. But of course many of the objects that we cherish are not things that we own or have any connection with except as an admirer. They are such objects as Manet's painting *Blonde Nude* or a sixteenth-

20

century French maiolica dish or the carved screen in the Chapel of Kings College, Cambridge, or merely a particular building listed by the National Trust. We need not cherish such objects because they enhance our status in our own estimation or because they increase our pride in our own achievements. Often they cannot, for as a foreigner our pride may, and can, only arise from the most remote source – being a member of the human race, for example, that is capable of such creation.

Moreover, a woman's attitude to her jewelry, or a man's attitude toward his favourite shotgun, may be a mixed one, partly that of satisfying the desires that arise from self-love and partly that of loving admiration. A woman may cherish a necklace, and admire its design and workmanship, long after she has ceased to own it and long after it has any direct connection with her life. The test of genuine love in such cases is simply that the love continues after all possible use of the object merely as a means to self-love ceases. Something of this interest in continued care can be seen in those advertisements that offer objects for sale 'only to a good home where they will be cared for properly'. Thus private ownership of an object does not exclude loving it for its own sake. In fact, love of an object is a common reason for later wishing to own it and thus ensuring its presence. If we did not first love objects – love them independently of our self-love – they could not later directly contribute to our self- love as they sometimes do. Objects that are not cherished by their owner cannot contribute directly to the owner's self-love and the satisfaction of the owner's desires however much the objects are admired by other people. Their admiration may stimulate that of the owner and thus enlarge the satisfaction of his or her self-love, but such possessions do so only indirectly as the object of other people's admiration. When that is absent, as it sometimes is, then the objects themselves are powerless to move the agent, for the agent cannot feel even pride of possession in objects that he or she does not at least like or admire. Cer-

21

tainly, they cannot satisfy the agent's self-love since the agent does not take them to be admirable ornaments. A person who glories in certain possessions may or may not also genuinely cherish them; proud ownership of objects neither ensures nor prevents love of them. Taking pride in their possession may arise either from loving them or from self-love. But even when pride of ownership is at first maintained solely by self-love, it may happen that the possessions eventually come to be cherished for their own sake. It may also happen that the owner's self-love is enhanced by pride in the value judgments the owner makes of the objects that are loved.

It is a psychological commonplace that children cannot love themselves – cannot develop a sense of self-worth – unless they are first attracted toward, and identify with, such satisfying external objects as the mother's breast. Unless children can invest their affection in external objects, they cannot invest it in themselves. The crucial importance of object-love for the development of appropriate self-love is illustrated in psychoanalytic terms by Karl Abraham's discussion of the significance of the agent's ability to transfer libido to other objects, both animate and inanimate. Thus Abraham writes of the paranoid schizophrenic:

The patient whose libido has turned away from objects has set himself against the world. He is alone, and faces a world which is hostile to him. It seems as though his ideas of persecution were directed especially against that person upon whom he had at one time transferred his libido in a marked degree. In many cases, therefore the persecutor would be his original sexual object.

The auto-eroticism of dementia praecox is the source not only of delusions of persecution but of megalomania.... The mental patient transfers on to himself alone as his only sexual object the whole of the libido which the healthy person turns upon all living and inanimate objects in his environment, and accordingly his sexual over-estimation is directed toward himself alone and assumes enormous dimensions. For he is his whole world. (1942, pp. 74–5)

Clearly, we can treat libido as the disposition to give and receive affection rather than, as Abraham did, purely sexual energy. In doing so we can still appreciate the force and accuracy of Abraham's remarks about the schizophrenic process: The agent 'carries his self-isolation so far that in a certain measure he boycotts the external world. He no longer gives it anything, or accepts anything from it. He grants himself a monopoly for the supply of sense-impressions'. (p. 75) Thus if our love of inanimate objects were, as Taylor claims, not genuine love at all but simply love of self, the withdrawal of this self-love from mere objects should not produce megalomania. For if objects are attractive only because they satisfy the agent's self-love, then withdrawal of love from the objects, and the consequent loss of ornaments, presumably diminishes rather than strengthens self-love. So if Abraham's view of the effects of transference of libido to the self is correct, that of Taylor must be mistaken.

It is obvious that we can cherish particular situations, activities, achievements, accomplishments, capacities, principles, and beliefs in addition to animals and people. We can cherish all these different things because we can value them in themselves, independently of their use as means to other ends. Thus we can hold dear, and feel deep affection for, the house in which we were reared, a particular performance of Handel's opera *Saul*, the mathematical ability of Leibniz, the biological research project in which we are engaged, our country's international cultural reputation, and the belief in Christ as the Redeemer of mankind. In all these cases we can substitute the word 'love' for 'cherish' simply because we take what is being cherished as something that is held dear – loved – because it is valued for itself. No such inference can be made if we substitute the word 'like' for 'cherish'. To like our family home, or to like a performance of *Saul*, may or may not be to hold it dear, to love it as worthwhile in itself. Sometimes it is, of course, and then we are using 'like' and 'love' as synonyms. Quite commonly, we are not; and then we are distinguishing, on the one hand, between liking in the sense of enjoying, wanting, preferring, or choosing, and on the other hand, cherishing or loving. When we do so, what we love is something that we value for itself even though we may believe some aspects of the object to be worthless. But as we shall argue later, it does not follow that what we do love must be only other qualities of the object – that the loved object must consist in a complex of specifiable qualities.

Now we could not properly claim that we loved a particular set of means but only as means, that we loved them as long as – and only as long as – they filled that role. For then we should be asserting that we were attached to whatever filled that role independently of the special character of its occupant. In that case, our love would be directed neither at the occupant nor at the role itself: not at a specific occupant, certainly, because any occupant would serve as well as any other; and not at the role itself because love of that role could consist only in valuing a specific type of means simply because any instance of it led us to our goal. But then the same objection would arise as in the case of specific instances – or specific occupants of the role – namely, that to value a type or role in this way is not to cherish any of its features except its effectiveness in helping us to obtain our end. Any equally effective type, like any equally effective instance of that type, would be equally valued, and hence substitutable for any other. However, to love someone in particular or to love some specific thing is to value the person or object as a unique individual with its own worth, and thus to value the person or object as irreplaceable in one's affections. It is not to commit oneself to loving whatever other person or object possesses the same merits or relevant qualities, and in particular, to loving a substitute of equal or greater effectiveness. This is another way of asserting that in love of the particular the agent values the beloved as being inherently worthwhile. Nothing else will do in its place. Yet from this it does not follow that we can love – really love – only people or animals. In order to obtain that conclusion we must take 'love' to mean only 'be in love with', and that is a stipulative definition for which good reasons would have to be, but have not yet been, given.

Of course, it is often said that because we can only love what possesses an individual character, what is loved must have individual interests that we can identify with our own. Anthony Quinton, for example, has argued that only personalities, even if incomplete, can have interests and hence be objects of love. For in loving a person one must be able to think of that person 'as a continuing being with an identity like one's own'. Some of the persons or quasipersons, such as animals, infants, and defectives, whom we love cannot, therefore, reciprocate our love, although they can like us. The characteristics that Quinton takes to be constitutive of personality are 'consciousness, rationality, will, moral status and capacity for personal relations'. Each of these characteristics can display a weak form: Thus there can be mere consciousness of pain without consciousness of a continuing self; practical rationality displayed in the selection of means to ends; behaviour motivated by desire but not by deliberated choice; moral patients who are not moral agents; capacity to respond to, but not to identify with, another personality. Objects that do not possess even these restricted features are not individual personalities with interests of their own. Because of this, we cannot identify ourselves with their interests, and for that reason love of nonpersons cannot arise. (1973, pp. 104–5)

Against this it can be said that a thing's possession of a distinctive or individual character does not depend on that thing possessing interests. The eighteenth-century colour print entitled *The Sacred White Horse* by the Japanese artist Harunobu is highly individual, indeed unique, but it has no moral or legal rights and claims, or wants, to which we must attend. It is desecration to deliberately damage such works of art, yet this is not because they have wants, rights, and interests that are being violated. Those belong to the people associated with them: their creators, their owners, and their audience. In cherishing works of art, we also cherish the distinctive abilities of their creators, but these abilities and talents do not themselves have wants, rights, and interests. Those are attributable only to the people who possess the talents. We take works of art, like many other things, to be inherently worthwhile and hence suitably cherished. Because we cannot fall in love with them – for we cannot identify their wants and interests with our own – it does not follow that we cannot try to preserve them, wish to be in their presence, admire and delight in them, that they cannot deeply move us, that we cannot feel attached to them: in brief, that we cannot feel genuine affection or love for them despite the fact that they lack the status of agents who have intrinsic worth simply by being agents.

LOVING CARE AND BENEVOLENCE

Sometimes in cherishing people we develop a passion for them in all their aspects; sometimes we devote ourselves wholeheartedly to furthering their welfare, and take pleasure in their company, while feeling no special tenderness toward them; and sometimes we simply show loyal, unselfish, and benevolent concern for the good of people whom we have never met. All these varieties of behaviour are commonly referred to as forms of caring. What they have in common is disinterested care – care that is given for the benefit of the recipient and not merely for our own advantage. Yet why should this sometimes be called a type of 'love'? Nurses in hospitals, medical practitioners in their surgeries, welfare workers, and teachers of disadvantaged children often give disinterested care, but we do not say that it is usually given either from love or for love of their clients. We introduce the term 'love' in this usage only when the care is not required by the nature of the social role itself, when neither duty nor personal advantage is operative. To do something for some-

26

one for love, or out of love, is at the very least to extend care simply because it appears to benefit the recipient without being required of the donor, and to do this simply because of the feelings of goodwill the agent has for the recipient. It is to exhibit the sort of care that is a necessary but not sufficient condition of the relationship of love. It is insufficient because this sort of care, as Aristotle points out, is a defining feature of friendly feeling. In the *Rhetoric* he writes, 'We may describe friendly feeling towards any one as wishing for him what you believe to be good things, not for your own sake but his, and being inclined, so far as you can, to bring these things about'. (1984, 1381a 35–8, p. 2200) Because there are different degrees of good will, there are different degrees to which we wish to benefit the recipients of our care, just as there are different kinds of care appropriate to different sorts of recipients. We can reasonably wish to comfort a person but not our dearly loved drawing by Grunewald; we can wish to be approved of and cared for by our lover, or by God, but not by a work of art. We can try, with some success, to preserve a work of art in its original physical condition, but we cannot do this to a spouse.

However, although benefiting the recipient is something we can do for people, animals – and by analogy, objects – it does not seem to be applicable to activities. Who or what is the beneficiary of my love of tennis? In playing it with great pleasure, am I making either the game or myself a recipient of my disinterested care? Playing the game is the object of my desire, and my enthusiasm for the game and devotion to it may show that I care about, or like and enjoy, the activity for its own sake. This would not be true if I played merely for the exercise or merely as a social pastime. But there is no recipient or object of my disinterested care. If I were the object or beneficiary of my own care, it would not be disinterested. Either the care would be a means to some further end of mine or it would be directed toward my own satisfaction and advantage and be self-regarding. I might love for its own sake

27

the good health that my playing produced, but I should not love tennis. For me to love an activity is for me to care for, be attached to, desire to do, the activity itself. Nevertheless, my love of the activity is self-regarding since I act only for my own enjoyment. So benefiting a recipient for the recipient's sake alone is an instance of disinterested care; pursuing an activity for its own sake is not. True, in both cases our love consists in the devoted care that we give to the recipient or activity as an end in itself. But in the second case our love is directed only at our own pleasure and hence is not disinterested care.

All these features of our love of people, animals, and objects – its varieties, its basis of disinterested or devoted care, and its appraisal of inherent worth – would seem to be common knowledge and not subject to serious controversy. If this is so, it follows that love, even when confined to love between human beings, is not always a 'give-and-take relationship', whose participants will have desires that reflect this symmetrical relationship. Unrequited love is often but not invariably painful. There are people who can only feel affection for another person if the affection is not returned. They are able to admire, be concerned for, and take care of other people, but are unable to accept such care in return. They must be actors and not patients. We may classify such people as neurotic and their affection as a symptom of the neurosis. But the somewhat unsatisfactory role that the affection plays in their lives does not show that their affection is not genuine. It is genuine because, among other features, it incorporates the agents' desire for themselves to give disinterested care, and not merely the desire to have someone else extend such care on their behalf. Love for a person does not require that the lover have the desire to care for the beloved by the lover's own hand, for there are many reasons why the lover may not wish to do so – for example, because of anxiety, lack of self-esteem, and guilt. But when the desire is present, as in the case of those people who can give but not receive love, the desire to extend personal care is clearly an instance of their desire to bestow their disinterested care in the role of lover.

In any case, there is also hopeless love from afar, love that flourishes either in spite of, or because of, the lack of reciprocity. The love some children feel for parents who have rejected them is of the first sort; the unsatisfiable love described and advocated by the troubadours of Languedoc is of the second sort. Neither loving someone nor being in love with someone is a symmetrical relationship: Desires for association, communication, and reciprocity of affection are common but dispensable. What is indispensable is the agent's desire to give or receive disinterested care, and in the case of ardent love, the agent's wish to display or receive tender concern.

Benevolence, solicitude, and disinterested care differ from each other but overlap in some respects. What all three share with other sorts of love is the notion of helpful concern. But the kindly goodwill characteristic of the benevolent person need not develop into the attentive care displayed by the solicitous person or into the tender care expressed in ardent love. On the other hand, in the case of love between people it is not possible for one person to love another and yet never have goodwill toward the beloved, never wish to please him or her, never be pleased at that person's happiness, and never be other than neutral toward the good of the loved one. It is certainly possible to have a permanent sexual liaison without goodwill and hence love. It is also possible to have an enduring close relationship largely dependent for its maintenance on mutual dislike. Mr. and Mrs. Maclintick in Anthony Powell's novel *Casanova's Chinese Restaurant* are a case in point. The tenor of their married life is sufficiently revealed by the exchange between them in which Maclintick says:

'Moreland looks all right to me. What is wrong with him? Of course it was insane of me to express any opinion in front of a woman like you'.

'Go on', said Mrs. Maclintick. 'Just go on'.

'And what reason have you for saying Matilda isn't pleased?' said Maclintick. 'I only wish I had a wife with half Matilda's sense'.

'Matilda didn't seem to be showing all that sense when I was talking to her just now', said Mrs. Maclintick, still quite undisturbed by this unpleasant interchange, indeed appearing if anything stimulated by its brutality. (p. 149)

Of course, it is commoner to find relationships in which malice and hatred are closely intertwined with love, as in the case of Martha and George in Edward Albee's play *Who's Afraid of Virginia Woolf?* But if we ever are to be able to distinguish love from hate, the former must embody recognizable goodwill toward the beloved and the latter ill-will toward the victim. A lover who over the long term wished only ill-will toward his consort would be as much a definitional absurdity as a man who, filled with hate for his consort, could wish her only good. To love someone — to value the person for his or her own sake — implies wishing to benefit the person and advance the person's welfare; otherwise, the lover would not be valuing the person as an individual agent with his or her own goals, projects, needs, and desires. To the extent that the agent does not wish to advance the welfare of the beloved we are entitled to infer that the agent's attitude contains other, and conflicting, elements. On the other hand, because a person may be capable of giving love but be unable, for psychological reasons, to accept it in return, there is no logical absurdity in the case of a lover not caring about being well treated and valued by the beloved. It is a fact that some people can love others only if their affection is returned with ill-will, contempt, and punishment. These cases make it clear that even though a relationship of love between people ordinarily consists in each partner wishing both to receive affection and to give it, this need not always be so. Some people can only receive affection; other people can only extend it. Nevertheless, even passive partners are essential to some forms of love.

There is, according to Leila Tov-Ruach, another necessary feature of love: it is what she calls 'intensely focused attention' or 'formative attentive regard'. This is attention that both concentrates on and helps to form and maintain those traits of a person that the person takes as constitutive of his or her character. (1980, p. 468) Certainly it is true that it is not possible for one person to cherish another without paying some attention to some of the character traits of the beloved. A mother who claims to love her daughter but actually has no opinion as to whether her daughter is loyal, trustworthy, greedy, hot-tempered, affectionate, vicious, deceitful, fearful, melancholy, or brave, is not simply unobservant or dull. She does not care; she has no interest in her daughter, and has shown this by paying no attention to any of the traits that constitute her daughter's character. But it is not possible for us to love someone in whom we take no interest, for without interest there can be no concern, liking, admiration, attraction, committal, or benevolence, and if none of these is present there is no basis for a claim of love. On the other hand, it is possible to like someone or something without being very interested in the person or the object. I can meet someone at a party and take an immediate liking to him because he represents a kind of person that I always like. But I need not remember him for very long or even wish to meet him again: My interest in him may be exhausted by the one occasion on which I met and liked him. Similarly, when I hear a familiar quintet of Boccherini's I may register my mild approval without pausing to give it my full attention. It does not, and perhaps never has, greatly caught my interest though I like what I hear. Again, I may be firmly committed to various causes – preservation of rain forests, aboriginal welfare, elimination of the heroin traffic – without being deeply interested in learning much about any of them. They are simply duties to which I am committed because of my more general political and social views.

Of course, it is common for mothers genuinely to love their daughters while giving little attention to the particular traits thought by the latter to be of special importance in their own characters. An adolescent girl's belief that her own most characteristic and valuable qualities are kindliness and loyalty may not be shared by her mother. So it does not follow that the mother's attentive regard will be directed at just those traits that her daughter thinks are central in her own character. If the two women openly disagree on this point and neither convinces the other, then the focused attention given by the mother cannot help to form and maintain such traits in the daughter. Because of this, it cannot be correct to suggest, as Tov-Ruach does, that the recipient of focused attention 'could not retain those traits outside of the particular attentional relation'. (p. 468) When the traits on which attention is focused are not those thought to be important by the recipient, she will argue, sometimes rightly, that her character has been misinterpreted, that the attention fastened on her has been misdirected, and that consequently the attention she received has no bearing on the formation and retention of her central traits. Hence we can conclude that although attentive regard, like benevolence, is a necessary condition of love between human beings, formative attentive regard is not.

The only other necessary feature of this sort of love is affection in the sense of tender, rather than merely disinterested, care. A person can display disinterested care out of a sense of religious duty without displaying any affectionate sensitivity to the individual character of the recipient. If this special consideration is absent the relationship cannot be one of personal love; the recipient is not being singled out by the agent for attentive regard and is not being given a special favourable place in the agent's estimation. When there is no such regard and position there is nothing to distinguish the relationship from that of benevolence – a relationship that, in principle, could include any number of peo-

32

ple. A relationship of affectionate care, on the other hand, is limited in its number of participants by the limitations imposed by the requirements of interest, attention, committal, and intimacy. Because we cannot be equally interested in, attentive to, committed to, and intimate with, a large number of people, we cannot enter into relationships of equally affectionate care with them. To have close and affectionate relationships with a few people ensures not having such relations with any larger number.

LOVE-COMPRISING RELATIONS AND PUBLIC CRITERIA

Writing of sexual love between people, W. Newton-Smith has argued that once we agree on the necessary features of sexual love we need not agree on much else about it. There are, he says, 'love-comprising relations' such as caring, liking, respecting, committal, benevolence, and attraction, that are neither 'jointly necessary' nor completely dispensable. Different people 'require them to be satisfied to different degrees before awarding the epithet love to a relationship'. Because there are no objective public criteria as to their required degree of satisfaction, these love-comprising relations do not provide us with a positive test for the existence of love. That is, they do not provide us with sufficient conditions for its presence. People simply disagree as to the importance they give to the satisfaction of these different features of sexual love. (1973, pp. 128–30) Hence they differ considerably as to the sorts of actions that lovers may be expected – and ought – to take; and thus people create different types of social institutions in which those various sorts of actions are given systematic expression. (p. 133)

All this is true. But all these claims are true, also, of many other concepts, especially moral ones such as honesty, loyalty, courage, generosity, and greed. The same can be said of Newton-Smith's love-comprising relations themselves: knowing, caring, liking, respecting, attraction, affection, committal, benevolence. None of these psychological con-

33

cepts has objective public criteria for its presence – that is, identifying and sufficient criteria applicable to every case. There are no standardized tests that we can apply in order to determine whether Max genuinely likes or esteems or is attracted by Mini, and whether he likes her slightly or a great deal. Each of these relations can be given expression in many different ways, and these vary according to the personality of the agent, the circumstances of the occasion, and the conventions of the local group. In spite of that, within a particular situation and a particular society, there is usually no great difficulty in people reaching agreement as to whether a given action shows any, some, or much esteem, affection, benevolence, or commitment. Love is no different in this respect. When people who are in a position to make an informed judgment nevertheless disagree on a marginal or novel case, and on the depth of the relationship, they still agree on the general run of cases because members of their group have been educated to do so. If the situation were otherwise, the social group would eventually disintegrate since much, although not all, of its daily activities require such agreement if they are to be carried out successfully. The existence of welfare legislation and the enforcement of family law both reflect this agreement and help to strengthen it. To some extent we do enforce legal standards of care in the cases, for example, of children, the ill, and the aged. We have laws that provide for commitment in marriage by limiting divorce, or that guard our privacy and reputations and hence maintain respect for us in the community. The habitual enforcement of such laws helps to create something like public standards – objective public criteria – for the interpersonal relationships, such as respect, care, and committal, with which they deal.

It is true, of course, that within any social group in a large modern society people will differ as to which form of sexual love they prefer: that of respect, constancy, and commitment, for example, or that of passion, desire, and risk. But the institutions and public opinion of these societies also differ

34

in the extent to which they favour and support different forms of love and different sorts of partners. This being so, it is not surprising that when different forms of sexual love are not distinguished by us, the result is that we disagree as to the importance we should confer on the satisfaction of the various components of that love. However, when two octogenarians marry, most observers can agree that the two are in love despite the fact that their physical attractiveness and sexual desire for each other may be limited. In the same way, there can be general agreement everywhere that the Greek man who endangers his own life in order to save his daughter from a collapsed building, the African woman who risks starvation so that her working husband may eat, the American wife who continually exhausts herself at an unpleasant job so that her husband can finish his university education, are all clear examples of sacrifices made from love. Thus when we single out a specific form of love, and its particular components, we have little difficulty in finding uncontroversial instances of it. That we can also find more difficult cases – for example, the middle-aged wife who no longer feels sexual desire for her husband and asks herself whether she still loves him – certainly does not show that people in general always disagree on the importance of the various elements of sexual love, or those of any other form of love.

LOVE, INFATUATION, AND EVALUATION

The problem of identifying cases of genuine love certainly arises when we attempt to distinguish between love and infatuation. Because infatuation is extravagant or foolish love, an infatuated person, quite commonly, is someone who in over-valuing the beloved has mistaken beliefs concerning her or him. The infatuated man does not realize that his beloved wants only his status. In consequence of his over-valuations the infatuated man has poor grounds for believing that his desires can be satisfied by the loved one or that the desires

35

of the beloved can be satisfied by him. However, Gabrielle Taylor has tried to draw a different distinction between infatuation and love, a distinction based on two different sorts of wants. One sort requires the agent to evaluate favourably what the agent wants: 'his wanting *a* is based on the thought that *a* is of some value to do or have'. With the other sort of want the agent

may not evaluate *a* at all; or he may think that no value or even that a dis-value attaches to doing or having *a*; and finally he may think it worth while to do or have *a*, but if so then not because *a* as such is worth doing or having, but because he thinks it worth while to satisfy his desires, either on this occasion or as a general policy. (1976, p. 155)

Given this distinction, Taylor believes that perhaps the wants of the loving person are 'based on the thought that it is worth while *e.g.*, to be with and cherish *y*', whereas the wants of the infatuated person lack this feature. She also believes that it may be very difficult in any given case to distinguish between the two sorts of wants because they exist together and one often turns into the other. (p. 155)

Now it is indisputable that we sometimes want, or want to do, what we judge by our own standards to be inferior, tawdry, degrading, harmful, second-rate, despicable, disgusting, or generally unworthy of us. Perversions such as fetishism, exhibitionism, voyeurism, and various forms of sadism are examples of this. The agent may disapprove of his or her behaviour even while indulging in it. The same is often true of addictions to alcohol, drugs, and gambling. The last of these, Otto Fenichel argues,

is a provocation of fate, which is forced to make its decision for or against the individual. Luck means a promise of protection (of narcissistic supplies) in future instinctual acts. But what is more important is that the typical gambler consciously or unconsciously believes in his right to ask for special protection by fate. His gambling is an attempt to compel fate in a magical way to do its duty. (1946, p. 372)

Yet the gambler may realize this to be futile. Sometimes we know why we are compelled to engage in activities of which we disapprove and sometimes we have no insight into the reasons why we have such desires. It is also indisputable that on occasion we simply want something, perhaps on impulse, and apply no standard to it, do not consider what value we should place on the object if we were to make a judgment. An extreme case of this is kleptomania. In it 'we take possession of things which give the strength or the power to fight supposed dangers, especially . . . loss of self-esteem or of affection. Its unconscious formula is: "If you don't give it to me, I'll take it." '(p. 370) Still, it is highly disputable whether facts such as these can be used to distinguish between infatuation and love.

Suppose that we confine ourselves to considering only examples of love between people. Then it is obvious that many cases of infatuation in love, far from being instances of negative evaluation or nonevaluation, are instances of over-valuation. The infatuated lover exaggerates the charms of the beloved, the depth of their feeling for one another, the extent of their common interests. Or if the lover does not exaggerate such matters of fact, he or she exaggerates the value that each person places on the other's company, or over-values the beloved's modest signs of wit, amiability, and sensitivity. Common qualities and ordinary performance are praised as outstanding. This love is not so much blind as undiscriminating and humble. As Freud put it: 'the ego becomes more and more unassuming and modest, and the object more and more sublime and precious, until at last it gets possession of the entire self-love of the ego, whose self-sacrifice thus follows as a natural consequence. The object has, so to speak, consumed the ego'. As a result of this, says Freud, 'the functions allotted to the ego ideal entirely cease to operate. The criticism exercised by that agency is silent; everything that the object does and asks for is right and blameless. Conscience has no application to anything that is done for the sake of

37

the object.' What has happened, Freud concludes, is that '*The object has been put in the place of the ego ideal*'. (1953, p. 113) Thus Oscar Wilde thought that a man whom he loved, Lord Alfred Douglas, had written a pair of 'exceedingly beautiful poems' in 'Two Loves' and 'In Praise of Shame'. Yet the only feature that distinguishes them from other juvenilia of the period is their expression of homosexual yearnings of a grossly sentimental kind. In such cases as this it is not that the agent has neurotically chosen as his love-object someone whom he judges to be inferior and unworthy. Rather it is that he has been swept away by blind desire in which there is no considered evaluative judgment pro or con but merely undiscriminating over-valuation.

There are, in fact, various types of infatuation, and one of them, as in the case of falling in love, is certainly that in which the agent is carried away, without insight or proper evaluative judgment, by blind desire – that is, by desire that results from forces in the agent of whose character he is unaware. A closely related type is that in which the agent is compelled by a desire or craving over which the agent has no control, for reasons that the agent may or may not understand, to want, or even to love, what the agent regards as unworthy in certain respects – as something that the agent would prefer not to want or to love. The agent's evaluation of what is wanted or loved may well be sound although the craving or love remains unaffected by it. The person in this situation is foolishly infatuated because weak-willed. A third type is that of the agent who exhibits bad judgment and misvaluation for reasons such as ignorance and recklessness. What is common, however, to these three types of infatuation is clearly not the absence of favourable evaluation. It is, rather, the agent's inability to scrutinize his or her desire critically – an inability seen by Freud, in the case of love, as the result of the replacement of the ego ideal by the beloved. This inability has two components: either the inability to form sound appraisals of fact or of value, or the inability to affect the craving by any appraisals and judgments once made, or both. These, then, form the difference between the passion of infatuation and the passion of thoughtful love. To the extent that a lover is infatuated by the beloved, the lover is unable to act and feel, because of these constraints, according to the requirements of sound judgment. Although on occasion the lover's appraisals may be correct and the desire well placed, this will be the result of happy chance, or of unconscious mechanisms, and not of the guidance of considered evaluation.

THE LOVER'S JUDGMENT OF WHAT IS LOVED

It does not follow from the difference between infatuation and love that one person loves another only if the beloved is believed to possess certain qualities that the lover values favourably and thoughtfully. The agent can love the beloved, as Taylor points out, even though the lover cannot specify such features and qualities when asked to do so. A man can be attracted to a woman without believing that she has some attractive characteristics that provide his reason for loving her. But the fact that the agent is attracted to her, and loves her, for reasons that he is unable to articulate by identifying specific qualities, does not show that he is infatuated. He may merely be poor at analyzing her character or the relationship between his character and hers. Even so, he can still respond to her as a whole; and his desire for her company and for the maintenance of their relationship may be the outcome of his considered judgement. The soundness of his judgment – his ability to make sound appraisals and have them influence his wants – does not depend on his ability to analyze the character and personality of his beloved into the elements that he believes have attracted him to her. The conclusions of such analyses are often mistaken: The agent believes that it is his wife's independence and vigour that attracts him whereas it turns out, on closer scrutiny, that it is her maternal dominance and her ability to express his own forbidden impulses that appeal to him. Yet when this is brought to his notice there is no guarantee that he will be convinced of its truth; or if convinced, that he will find these qualities as attractive as the ones that they replace.

There is, then, a general question as to the connection between the characteristics in their loved ones that lovers claim have attracted them and the characteristics that may have actually appealed to them. Hence there is also a further question as to whether these latter characteristics, if known, would be evaluated favourably by the agent. It is not difficult to find, in the divorce courts, cases in which the couple admit that only after a period of psychological therapy did they become aware of the real reasons why they had been attracted to each other, and that once these reasons had been revealed, the couple no longer wished to remain married. Of this kind of relationship Lawrence Kubie remarks:

The story is all too familiar of maladjusted young people who try to escape their separate miseries by joining their problems in marriage. Since marriage never cures a neurosis, it usually ends up by being blamed for it; and presently the neurotic angers of both partners are pitted against each other in a merciless battle. Even if this battle can be checked by analysis, the couple may find that with the elimination of the original neurotic reasons for the marriage no healthy reason remains for continuing together. (1960, p. 172)

But underlying this question of the agent's evaluation of those features of the partner that actually influenced the agent is a more general problem, one whose answer determines the importance we attach to our question about evaluation. The problem is simply this: Do people always love one another simply because they value each other's traits? It is widely believed that they do, and Gabrielle Taylor has put the suggestion thus:

If x loves y, then x wants to benefit and be with y, etc., and he has these wants (or at least some of them) because he believes y has some determinate characteristics x in virtue of which he thinks it worthwhile to benefit and be with y. He regards satisfaction of these wants as an end and not as a means toward some other end. (1976, p. 157)

One weakness of this suggestion, as we have already noted, is that some agents do not have, and so cannot report, such beliefs about the determinate characteristics of those whom they love. When questioned, these agents can list the characteristics that they like or admire in the person whom they love. But they often do not claim, and it does not follow, that these characteristics are what make the agents love their partners. In any case, of those agents who do claim to have love-inducing beliefs of this kind, we can always properly ask, as we have seen, whether the beliefs are both correct and well grounded. There is no reason why we must accept the agent's account of why he or she loves someone: The agent may be self-deceived, emotionally confused, or mistaken for a variety of other reasons.

WHAT DOES THE LOVER LOVE?

It is a genuine question, then, whether one person can love another merely because of valuing particular qualities of the beloved – his or her honesty, courage, generosity, affectionate disposition. For if this is so, then it seems to follow that anyone else who possesses these qualities would be equally worthy of love by the agent. The mixture of qualities might in fact be peculiar to the loved one, or the lover might simply believe it to be unique. In practice, of course, it might be unique to the small range of that person's potential partners. Nevertheless, in principle the agent would seem to be committed to loving equally well anyone else who possessed that same combination of qualities. How, then, can the agent love a person for that person's self alone – for something distinctive of the beloved? To this it will commonly be replied either that the agent cannot – that other than the qualities of the beloved there exists nothing distinctive to be the object of

41

love – or that the agent does not love the beloved because of determinate qualities alone, that is, the specific types of courage, generosity, and affection that the beloved displays. Now it may be asserted, on this first view, that the agent loves because of the manner in which the beloved instantiates or embodies these determinate characteristics. It is this woman's instantiation of them that the lover finds attractive and worthwhile. Her special tone of voice when being generous, the unique emphasis given by her repeated gestures of affection, her inimitable ability to invent ways of making herself be brave in the face of adversity – these are some of the features that the lover values and finds attractive; and they, either singly or in combination, are distinctive of her.

However, this answer still leaves us with the problem of what it is exactly that the agent loves. It is not, we said, merely the specific types of courage, honesty, affection, and generosity that the beloved displays. For in that case the beloved would be cherished because, and only as long as, he or she displayed those qualities. If so, then the agent must cherish the beloved only as the source and bearer of an itemizable set of determinate characteristics. The remainder of the beloved's characteristics, because they do not contribute to the agent's thinking 'it worthwhile to benefit and be with her', are not what he values in her. In this sense, the agent merely loves part of a person, not the entire woman. On the other hand, if the agent loves her even when she does not display her worthwhile characteristics – when she has altered temporarily or even permanently – what is it in her that the agent then loves? Is it her ability sometimes to display her worthwhile characteristics? If that is lost, can the agent love her only for what she once was? In the former case, the agent certainly loves only that part of her that consists in particular abilities, and the agent must love her only while she retains the abilities. In the latter case, the agent loves her for once having possessed certain qualities. But in both cases, what the agent claims to love are qualities or abilities that might

42

well be possessed by other people who would be, for that reason, equally worthy of the agent's love. There would be nothing distinctive in principle about the object of the agent's affections, and hence nothing about the beloved that would be irreplaceable in those affections; and hence, as was argued previously concerning types of means and occupants of roles, no love of someone as uniquely valuable and worthwhile.

It does not help to give as a reply to this the answer that what is loved is the beloved's exemplification of certain characteristics rather than the characteristics themselves. This response does not deal with the problem of exactly what it is that the agent proceeds to evaluate concerning the instantiated qualities of the beloved. To value a quality such as quick-wittedness wherever found is one thing; to value Maria's form of it is another. The reasons why I value quick-wittedness or frankness wherever I find them are not, presumably, the exact same reasons why I value Maria's quick-wittedness and frankness. For if they were, I should have no reason to love her and not love everyone else who possessed these qualities. Yet in fact it is only Maria whom I claim to love because she has them. Why is that? It cannot be simply that she has them to a greater degree than anyone else available or known to me. I can still love Maria, and not Ann, even after discovering that my friend Ann is franker and more quick-witted. There must, then, on this view, be something valued by me in the particular ways in which Maria's frankness and quick-wittedness show themselves in her thought and behaviour. These manifestations must not only have a different value for me from the manifestations of the same qualities by Ann, but the former must lead me to love Maria and the latter not lead me to love Ann. What can make this difference?

One answer might be that Maria's manifestations occur in complexes of other instantiated qualities that, taken all together, simply appeal to me – answer to my wants, or perhaps needs – for reasons of my psychological history, more than do Ann's manifestations of frankness and quick-wittedness. But this answer alters the original response, for it asserted that I loved Maria because of the way in which she instantiated particular qualities or displayed specifiable characteristics. The new answer suggests that what I value is more than that: I value a particular complex of instantiated qualities, and the original characteristics form only part of this complex. The beloved instantiates those original characteristics in conjunction with others that provide their setting. The original characteristics are not worthwhile to the lover and attractive by themselves; what makes them so is their being present in a complex that is both worthwhile and attractive to him while being distinctive of his beloved. Thus a woman whose emotional passivity expressed an appealing submissiveness might also be intellectually sympathetic, loyal, and stoical. This combination, when instantiated in specific ways by a petite, black-haired, and active woman, might prove to be irresistible to a suitor who would not be strongly drawn to any of these features taken singly.

Concerning this answer we can make two remarks. One is that although the answer enlarges on what instantiation amounts to, the answer does not avoid any of the criticisms made earlier. We still have to deal with the same issues. In principle, anyone who possessed the same instantiation- complexes of frankness and quick-wittedness as Maria would be equally worthy of my love. She would still be valued only as the bearer and source of an itemizable set of complex characteristics, and the remainder of her instantiations would not be counted in my love for her. Since I should love only some aspects of her, it would not be true to say that I loved the entire woman: If those aspects changed so would my love for her. Yet against this, people sometimes continue to love a person who, as a result of illness or accident, is completely changed in important respects. Do they love the person only because of a past relationship? If so, what exactly is it in the person that the agent then loves? An answer to this question will be given later.

44

The other remark to be made is that no answer in terms of instantiation can, in the nature of the case, shed any light on the difference between loving a person and loving that person's manifestation of certain qualities or properties – loving some of that person's characteristics. Yet there does seem to be such a distinction since we can love the latter without loving the former. Nor does this answer tell us how loving these characteristics leads us to love a particular person who possesses them rather than making us confine ourselves to loving those in whomever they are found. Neither does any such answer militate against the opposing view that we first love a person for his or her individual worth and then discover in the person some characteristics, some instantiated qualities, that we like; and that we can then mistakenly employ both as the explanation of, and justification for, our love. The fact that a lover helps to create in the loved one the features that the lover hopes to find, and that the lover values, suggests that quite commonly it is the agent's love that makes the lover believe, truly or falsely, that the beloved exemplifies, or could exemplify, particular qualities in a unique way.

In making this point, S. L. Goldberg has instanced the case of the princess in the fairy tale who kissed the toad and thus changed it back into a prince. For her to see the potential prince in the toad requires, he writes, 'a trust, a faith, not just in the existence and value and strength of certain potentialities in the other person, but also in one's own need, capacity and commitment to appreciate those potentialities and thereby perhaps help them realize themselves'. (1983, pp. 38–9) So in committing herself to the belief that there is a prince in the toad, the princess both reveals her love for the potential man – the man without existing qualities – and shows us that she relies upon her own capacity to help actualize the potential man in the toad. But if this is true of some cases of love, then Taylor's characterization of love cannot be: It cannot be a necessary condition of x loving y that the former believes the latter has specific features in virtue of which x thinks it worthwhile to benefit and be with y. On the contrary, it is sometimes a necessary condition of x believing that y has these specific features that x loves y. It is because of this love that x thinks it worthwhile to benefit and be with y.

2

Sexual desire

SEXUAL DESIRE AS THE WISH FOR PHYSICAL CONTACT

Normal sexual desire, says Alan Goldman, is 'purely the desire for contact with another person's body and for the pleasure which such contact produces'. The desire for such contact is both sufficient and necessary to make the desire sexual; and this physical contact, rather than the feelings and emotions that the contact might express, is 'the goal of sexual desire'. Activities that have only this goal – for example, kissing, embracing, and caressing under certain conditions – 'qualify as sexual, even without the presence of genital symptoms of sexual excitement'. (1976, pp. 268–9)

Now the desire for bodily contact, and for the pleasure that it produces, will certainly be a necessary condition of normal sexual desire if the word 'normal' is used to exclude all difficult cases. Scoptophilia – the expression of sexual desire by visual means alone – is an obvious example of the sort of activity that will be ruled out. Similarly, according to Goldman, such activities as voyeurism, masturbation, and the use of pornography, are simply substitutes for 'actual sexual contact'. (p. 270) So in the absence of the desire for bodily contact for its own sake there is no normal sexual desire. But given this definition, is it also the case that the desire only for physical contact, and for the pleasure that it brings, is a sufficient condition of normal sexual desire? The answer is not obviously 'yes'.

There are, for example, different sorts of physical contact. If two children devise a game that consists wholly in their running into each other with considerable force, the resulting

47

collisons may give them pleasure. They may even prefer to play this game only with each other and the goal of each need not be, to use Goldman's words, 'winning or exercising or knocking someone down or displaying one's prowess'. (p. 269) The goal for them is a certain kind of contact with the body of a particular person. Yet the desire for this contact and its pleasant consequences does not seem to be a case of sexual desire for each other's bodies. Their collisons do not seem to be a stage of, or substitute for, some recognizably sexual activity. It would be easy to devise games that did have such a character – games of body rubbing, for instance, that produced obvious signs of sexual arousal. But to characterize the desire for mere physical contact as sexual desire is to override the other pleasures of bodily contact. There is also the pleasure of muscular resistance to an external force, or that of being surprised by the unexpected sensations created by a sudden physical blow. The important point is that sexual desire, when it does aim at bodily contact, aims only at bodily contact that increases, or at least maintains, the sexual interest of the agent. Many forms of bodily contact do not: Two people who simply enjoyed pummeling each other for the tactile sensations they obtained might be sadomasochists but they would not be normal sexual partners. Hence the desire for mere physical contact, and for its pleasures, is not a sufficient condition of normal sexual desire.

There is a further qualification to be made concerning the definition both of sexual desire in general and normal sexual desire. It is that we can define 'sexual desire' either in terms of the bodily source of the physical sensations and mental activities that constitute and help to identify the desire, or in terms of the activity by which the desire is satisfied, or both together. Sexual sensations, sexual arousal, and also sexual desire, can arise from the stimulation of many areas of the human body, from many different kinds of situations – watching the sexual activity of other people, listening to pornographic accounts, reading to oneself, for example – and

48

from such activities as daydreaming or recalling past relationships. Similarly, the specific aims of sexual desires, that is, the activities in which the agent wishes to engage when he or she has a specific aim – and the agent need not – can be extremely various: sexual stimulation by whipping, the infliction of pain by sexual means, the intensification of sexual arousal through jealousy – these are common members of a very large set of practices. Any definition of 'sexual desire' that does not distinguish between the many different sources of sexual arousal as against the many different embodiments of sexual activity will be either too narrow or too wide for the purpose in hand.

Even if we accept Goldman's characterization of (normal) sexual desire, we have to realize that his characterization provides no test, in any given case, for distinguishing sexual desire from the other desires that frequently accompany it, desires for affection, admiration, reassurance, comfort, and security. These are among the many other desires that are sometimes present: the desire to release oneself from the ordinary constraints of social behaviour; or the desire to obtain unusual sensory experiences; and certainly the desire to exert the power both of dominating the partner and of biologically reproducing oneself. These desires lead to activity that stimulates, and in turn is stimulated by, sexual desire. It is a difficult question, therefore, how often pure sexual desire, of the sort described by Goldman, actually occurs, and how well we can recognize its presence. Tov-Ruach comments that men interpret sexual relations with women as 'an assurance of unconditional, unjudgmental attentive acceptance'. She goes on to assert that 'the excitement of adult male sexuality comes in part from the hope that sexual bonding will assure him what he had received in infancy from his mother: physical satisfaction from an unjudgmental other'. It is a point of interest, she says, 'that prostitutes report that their clients seem to want reassurance on their prowess even more than they want sex'. (1980, p. 482)

49

Again, what evidence we have on women's sexual behaviour indicates that a large majority of those surveyed have interpreted sexual intercourse chiefly as a means of expressing affection, intimacy, and feelings of security; and that enjoyment of intercourse for them depends on their belief in their partners' trustworthiness. (Fisher, 1973, pp. 398–9) Moreover, simple physical contact with another person's body for pleasure is not what takes place in cases of sexual perversion and displacement such as foot fetishism, pyromania, scoptophilia, and rituals of submission or domination. Since these are cases in which the desire for physical contact cannot be displayed and satisfied directly because it arouses anxiety, fear, and guilt, the substitute acts are complicated amalgams of various desires. Hence the sexual activity that these acts permit must express a variety of desires and emotions – the need for reassurance or the fear of sexual arousal, for example, or feelings of hate – rather than the mere desire for physical contact. But when we take all these exceptions into account, it looks as though unaccompanied, and supposedly 'normal', sexual desire may be relatively infrequent, and probably unimportant, in human sexual relations.

SEXUAL ACTIVITY INDEPENDENT OF LOVE

It is sometimes suggested that unadorned sexual activity has much to recommend it, and that the emotional and intellectual problems created by the presence of love, trust, admiration, and commitment could be eliminated if sexual activity were treated as a casual game, as an attractive recreation. As J.F.M. Hunter describes the case against these complications of physical pleasure, they make sexual satisfaction more difficult to attain; they make possible misunderstanding and deception; they bring together ill-assorted partners; and they produce grief and anger when partners change. He remarks that 'if we were as unromantic about sex as we are about eating, not only might we have more of it and enjoy it more, but there would be little or no place for the tensions, contrivances, jealousies and bitterness that now surround it'. (1983, p. 17)

But is any of this true? Not if what we have been suggesting is correct – that unaccompanied sexual desire plays a relatively small role in human social life. It is small because sexual desire is commonly an element in self-maintaining social systems – systems that help to create the character and expression of that desire. To turn sexual activity into a purely recreational pastime would be to alter drastically those systems and to produce new ones in which such notions as physical intimacy, game–partner, lover, and marital partner would be altered considerably. It would be to excise from sexual activity all its deeper psychological significance and much of its present social importance, including its connection with love. Yet all this is to be done for the sake of separating the less desirable consequences of love – tension, jealousy, bitterness – from the unalloyed pleasures of sexual desire. Even if we assume for the moment that such separation is possible and that purely sexual pleasures are prized by those who undergo them, it looks as though they will have to be found in a different set of partners from those who offer love and affection. For if the same partners offered both sexual recreation and sexual love to the same person, there would be no way in which the two forms of activity could be kept separate; each could, and would, influence the other. There would be a continuing struggle to keep the attitudes and emotions appropriate to one group from encroaching on those of the other group. In sum, the very attempt to remove tensions from sexual activity by making it purely recreational, proceeds on the assumption that sexual activity has a strong tendency to develop into sexual love unless prevented by institutional arrangements. Yet what could these be? The success of these arrangements would always be in serious doubt.

It may be objected, of course, that in saying this we pre-

51

judge the outcome of the proposed arrangements. But the basic point remains that the two groups would be competing for limited resources – the time and services of their members – in exactly the same way as a man's devotion to playing squash can compete with his wife's wish to have him at home. If someone had a recreational sex-partner, he or she would have to avoid, if possible, also having a love-partner at the same time. Otherwise, the competition between the two partners could well produce the tension that recreational sex was supposed to eliminate. On the other hand, having only one partner at a time would not solve the problem of having both recreation and love since they could not be kept from influencing – or perhaps contaminating – each other. However, once we envisaged two different and competing sets of partners, we should have to face the fact that people often become as attached to their recreational pastimes as they do to their work. In consequence, there is every reason to believe that recreational-partners and love-partners would simply find themselves, once again, in the familiar situation described by Arthur Schnitzler in his story *The Man of Honour* when the young man, Alfred, begins to tire of Elise, his working-class mistress.

He was the sort of man who was quite clever enough, and he flattered himself, considerate enough, not to let Elise notice these feelings of his, but, still they had the effect of making him once more frequent that comfortable middle-class society which he had almost deserted in the course of the last year. And when a very popular young lady, whom he met at a dance, the daughter of a wealthy manufacturer, treated him with marked friendliness, and he suddenly saw before him the promising possibility of an engagement suited to his position and means, he began to look on the other connection, which he had begun as a cheerful inconsequent adventure, as a burdensome fetter which a young man with his advantages should be able to shake off without hesitation. (pp. 83–4)

The difficulty, for Alfred, is to do it. Elise's trust, devotion, and confidence in him bring it about that Elise never believed herself more passionately adored by him as when he was fresh from some meeting with Adele, when, trembling still at the recollection of her sweet questioning glance, her thrilling touch, and, later, by the fragrance of their first secret lover's kiss, he came back to a home consecrated to him alone and to his faithless love: and every morning Alfred left his mistress, not with words of parting that he had composed outside the door, but with fresh protestations of eternal fidelity. (p. 84)

Conflicts of this sort are so common a topic in European literature that they should warn us of the problems created by the proposal to isolate the demands of sexual desire from the need for affection. The result of trying to do so, far from making sexual satisfaction less complicated and easier to obtain, is to make it more difficult because of the need to isolate it from the influences of family and working life. The truth is that the desire to unromanticize sexual relationships is itself one important element of a modern romance – that of sensual gratification that is trouble-free, free from the cares and responsibilities of ordinary personal intercourse.

Yet it is an ancient commonplace that a large part of the delight of lovemaking is not physical gratification. In Hunter's own words, we take joy

in being in a euphoric state quite unlike our normal condition, in being so unrestrainedly demonstrative, in having our attention completely focussed on and returned by someone we care for, in giving pleasure that shows so immediately and tangibly, in being able to express our attraction to another human being in such a sustained and concrete way, and in having that person accept and demonstrably exult in our interest. (1983, p. 12)

It is clear that most of these features cannot be present in a commercial sexual transaction, and it is highly unlikely that they can flourish in sexual activity of a purely recreational sort. For once we begin to care for a person and express our attraction to the person rather than express our appreciation of the person's body and physical performance, we are no longer merely playing a sexual game. We are initiating a personal relationship whose outcome is uncertain.

The distinction between sexual activity and love is commonly drawn as that between intense, limited, brief, and reiterated acts on the one hand, and milder, broader, and longer-lived forms of relationship on the other. In addition, it is often pointed out that sexual activity is a set of actions that can be entered into at will, whereas love is neither identical with a set of actions nor available on demand and terminable by request. We can urge someone to love his relatives, but all he can do in response is to show goodwill and try to find features in them by which he will be attracted. He may wish to feel more strongly toward them and yet find himself unable to do so. Conversely, he may try to resist being attracted and yet discover that he loves them. Love, it is said, has other differentiating features: it easily outlasts sexual activity, is always directed at a specific object whereas sexual desire can be free-floating, has many fewer people toward whom it is directed, and affects much larger areas of the personality to a much greater depth. For these reasons, sexual activity can be bought and sold; love cannot. We have to learn how to love people and objects, but we do not have to learn how to feel and express sexual arousal. Finally, we can love a wide variety of things, occasions, properties, animals, people, and activities. To only some of this variety can we feel sexual desire and direct our sexual activity.

Now it is certainly true that there are distinctions of these sorts to be drawn between love and sexual activity. But it is equally true that some of these distinctions need further examination. It makes an important difference, for example, whether we contrast all forms of sexual activity taken as a whole with all forms of love taken jointly, or whether we contrast sexual orgasm with the love of a child for its parents. The latter contrast is greater than the former. We do seem to have intense, limited, brief, and perhaps repeated, feelings

54

of love – momentary pangs – that often we have no difficulty in identifying. They are sudden, sharp feelings of affection and attraction, as when we realize in an instant how much we cherish and admire the person who has just spoken to us. We also have feelings of mild sexual desire that go on for long periods and are expressed in activities such as looking, reading, listening, and imagining rather than in bodily contact. If, then, we compare momentary pangs of love with momentary pangs of sexual arousal, or compare the gentler, long-term, and indirect forms of sexual desire with gentle signs of love and benevolent behaviour, the differences of intensity and duration between the two are not as striking as when we draw a contrast between a man's brief sexual encounter with a prostitute and the life-long love of that man for his son.

Similarly, the relationship of sexual activity to a set of associated actions is not so very different from that of love to such a set of actions. Neither sexual desire nor love need be expressed, or even acknowledged, by the agent. But when they are displayed, a very great variety of acts and actions can convey them without being identical with sexual desire or the disposition to love. Caressing a partner is one form of sexual activity but so is watching pornographic films and simultaneously caressing oneself. Loving care can also be expressed by watching someone, by listening to the person, or by leaving the person alone. The sense in which love consists partly in a disposition to pay a specific kind of sympathetic attention to the beloved is similar to the sense in which sexual desire also partly consists in a disposition to pay a specific kind of attention, that of sexual caressing, to its object. So while it is true that the various forms of love are not identical with, and thus exhausted by, various sets of specifiable actions, it is not true that sexual activity differs greatly in this respect.

Again, to feel sexual arousal and desire is to be in an agitated physical and mental state. Similarly, to feel love is to be in

55

an emotional state consisting in thoughts, sensations, and physiological changes; it is to be in a state of occurrent love rather than merely having the disposition to love. As William Lyons remarks, the agent has no basis for claiming to be in any emotional state unless he first believes that he 'is undergoing physiological changes caused by an evaluation (or appraisal) peculiar to some emotion'. (1980, p. 124) Correspondingly, the agent has no basis for claiming to be in a state of sexual desire unless he first believes that he is undergoing physiological changes – not necessarily genital ones – caused by some feature of his desire. In both cases, the agent tries to identify his state by locating the cause of his physical agitation. (p. 123) If he fails in the latter he cannot succeed in the former.

Of course, there are, in one sense, many more forms of loving care than there are forms of sexual activity, for we can make more types of things – people, animals, activities, places, for instance – the object of love than we can make the object of sexual desire; and loving care is itself a more complex relationship than is sexual activity. However, the former difference is one of number alone; it is the latter difference – that of complexity of relationship – that is significant. Loving care is a more complex relationship than purely sexual activity because, for one, love often incorporates sexual arousal and desire and adds their features to those of its own. But for another, even when love does not include sexual arousal and desire, it is directed, to some extent, at benefiting the beloved. To do this the lover must try to satisfy the needs and wishes, present and future, of the beloved for that person's sake and not merely for that of the lover. Someone who loves must try, therefore, to understand the character of the beloved and form some notion of how that character will bear upon, and be related to, his or her own. These requirements do not apply to simple sexual arousal. For arousal represents a need of the agent alone, and although its satisfaction often requires some cooperation from a partner, no attention need be paid to the fulfillment of that person's wishes. To the extent that such attention is given by the agent, its justification is instrumental: The agent's own pleasure and sexual satisfaction are increased by that of the partner. If, as in the case of sado-masochists, the agent's pleasure is not increased by satisfying the partner, then the agent has no sexual reason for trying to do so. An agent seized with lust, and only lust, rather than erotic love, is interested in bodies and not embodied persons. But the kinds of loving relationships possible between embodied persons include a range of attitudes, emotions, thoughts, and projects wholly absent from those between, per hypothesis, mere lusting bodies.

On the other hand, this fundamental difference between love and both sexual desire and arousal should not lead us to ignore some of their less obvious similarities. For example, one of the characteristics of love, other than mere benevolence, is that it is neither available on demand nor terminable at will. Of course, attentive care and consideration are often available for money, or on request from friends and relatives, or obtainable from people, such as hospital nurses, who have a duty to give it. Sometimes this sort of care, whether or not it is reciprocated, is transformed into liking or into love. But there are no actions that the agent can perform, no course of behaviour that the agent can adopt, and no form of self-persuasion that will produce the transformation. The best the agent can do is to follow a course of behaviour that will expose him or her to whatever influences can affect the relationship in the desired direction. Close interaction, attempts to understand another's character and needs, to be kind and sympathetic – these are efforts that the agent can make. Whether they lead to something more is beyond the agent's control.

Yet much the same holds true of feelings of sexual arousal and desire. It is true that priests urge their parishioners to love each other, but do not entreat their parishioners to feel sexual desire for each other, not even for their spouses. At most, priests advise reluctant wives to submit with good grace to their husbands' unwanted sexual advances. Yet this difference in priestly behaviour is surely not due to their belief that feelings of love are under the conscious control of the agent whereas feelings of sexual desire are not. Strictly speaking, neither is, although the agent's willingness to recognize the feelings, or to permit their public expression, depends upon the agent alone. People who occupy the social role of marriage-partner can reasonably be reminded of the thoughts and feelings and actions appropriate to that role, for in the marriage ceremony the bride and bridegroom have undertaken to try to maintain a relationship of loving care for each other. Priestly admonitions, then, can serve as reminders of past commitments that the agents should strive to fulfill; but the agents cannot guarantee their own success. Nor can they sensibly promise to love, in the future, a particular person whom they now love, and they certainly cannot sensibly promise to love someone whom they do not already love. They cannot even sensibly promise to like someone or something unknown to them except by description. What they can sensibly promise is to try to do these things. For liking and loving are never entirely the direct outcome of an agent's own efforts and wishes: propitious circumstances, the co-operation of other people, the presence of qualities and properties, thoughts and feelings, whose existence in the agent or other people cannot be forecast accurately – all these may be, and commonly are, required.

Hence sexual activity, arousal, and desire do not differ radically in this respect from liking and loving. The agent's fear, hatred, anger, or worry is capable, on occasion, of dissipating his sexual desire; sexual performance itself is affected by the appearance, emotions, and cooperation of the partners, by disturbing physical conditions, and by a host of other circumstances. Neither successful performance nor the existence of desire can be guaranteed merely by the agent's own efforts and wishes. The same is true of the cessation of sexual desire. A woman cannot sensibly promise to feel, or not to feel, sexual desire at a specific time and place, for an unknown man, and a man cannot sensibly promise to a woman that he will obtain, or give, complete sexual satisfaction – or that he will fail to give any – at a specific place. Whatever the claims of prostitutes, they cater only to a ready clientele, and even so offer no money-back guarantees. Sexual arousal and desire cannot always be summoned forth on demand and terminated at will. Their presence depends on many conditions beyond the control of the agents, and the fact that these conditions are taken into account by the participants in sexual activity indicates that such conditions are important. It is only because these conditions are so often satisfied that we overlook their necessity. The participants need to be in good health, not drunk or drugged or tired, not subject to public scrutiny and attempts at interference, not under immediate threat, and not distracted by unpleasant emotions. Moreover, in heterosexual activity, the man, at least, must be willing. When conditions such as these are not met, both desire and achievement may fail.

LEARNING TO EXPRESS LOVE AND SEXUAL DESIRE

What we are usually supposed to learn in learning how to love people and objects is appropriate love, the sort of love that is appropriate, according to some standard, for specific kinds of people or objects in particular circumstances and at particular times and places. People are not usually given lessons in how to feel attracted by someone and how to demonstrate affection for that person any more than they are explicitly taught how to be afraid, angry, or ashamed on certain occasions. They simply transfer their familial feelings, thoughts, and attitudes, without being explicitly taught, to people outside the family. For the most part, these transfers are reasonably successful since parents, relatives, and older siblings serve both as models for children and as sources of general information about such feelings as those of attachment. However, in those cases where no such opportunities for learning are available to a child – as a result of prolonged illness, for example, or institutional care or psychologically disturbed parents – therapeutic instruction may be required. The agent's inability to feel, or appropriately express, affection for other people and objects may need to be overcome by special means. This indicates that there is nothing strange, but merely uncommon, in people having to be explicitly taught and shown how affection arises, how trust is developed, and when and where love should be expressed. But it is not very uncommon. For the presence of large numbers of psychotherapists, psychologists, and counsellors in every western country testifies to a widespread belief that an even larger number of clients requires therapeutic education of their emotions. Nevertheless, the more common situation is that in which people are explicitly taught whom not to love sexually – certain classes of relatives and certain age-grades, for instance – and are warned against expressing affection on certain sorts of occasions, such as to official enemies in wartime, when it is considered to be dangerous, disloyal, or simply maladroit.

Yet in all these respects, the feeling and expression of love closely resemble the feeling and expression of sexual desire. Usually people do not have to be given instruction in how to feel sexual desire for someone else, although, as in the case of love, they may have to be taught something about its character and appropriate expression. Every society has social arrangements that presume, and cater for, the presence of sexual desire. But sometimes there are biological or psychological factors that inhibit or divert the development of normal sexual desire in a person, and he or she may be unable either to feel it or to express it in some socially appropriate fashion. Therapy and explicit instruction may be needed.

Thus the only difference, in respect of learning and instruction, between feelings of affection and feelings of sexual desire is that human beings have specifically sexual organs but no specific organs of beneficence and love. Of course, learning to make appropriate use of a sexual organ is a different sort of achievement from learning to form a relationship, such as that of appropriate love, with other people, although the former achievement may be part of the latter one. However, this difference in type of achievement is not an example of learning solely by physical maturation, on the one side, and learning solely by social maturation on the other. Since it is as easy to describe physically inappropriate uses of sexual organs, or sexual desire, as it is to describe socially inappropriate expressions of love, it is clear that both sexual desire and love require suitable objects. When directed at other people, both require suitable partners, and hence both require the participants to have a certain amount of information, which can only be socially acquired, as to how to proceed appropriately. Learning how to proceed in a purely sexual relationship is as much a social achievement as is learning how to proceed in a relationship of nonsexual love. While the former is a much simpler task than the latter, it is still possible to fail in the attempt through sheer ignorance of human physiology.

ADDITIONAL SIMILARITIES BETWEEN LOVE AND SEXUAL DESIRE

There are many additional similarities between love and sexual desire. The latter, like the former, can be felt at a distance without hope of requital; in both, a person can renounce the relationship while maintaining the feeling; in both the agent can make similar mistakes about the character of the object, the likelihood of the satisfaction of the agent's wants, and the importance to the agent of that satisfaction. With sexual desire, as with love, the agent can be mistaken as to his or her condition: The agent can mistake a desire for Ann's company as sexual desire just as the agent can mistake either of those

61

desires for that of the wish to give and receive loving care. Even if Goldman were correct in claiming that sexual desire is simply the 'desire for contact with another person's body and for the pleasure which such contact produces', an agent might believe that he or she wanted such contact and discover later, in a more intimate situation, that the desire had been for reassurance alone.

There are also other resemblances between love and sexual desire. Suppose we ask whether if Mini feels sexual desire for Max, she must believe that he has 'some recognizably attractive characteristics'. Can she feel drawn to him by sexual desire while finding that all his known characteristics are unattractive to her and that she is unable to say why she feels as she does? The obvious, though uncommon, answer is yes, she can, for she can be subject to dispositions in herself of whose nature she is unaware and whose force and causes, therefore, she cannot subject to rational scrutiny. In this respect, sexual desire and love are similar. It is not a necessary condition of X feeling sexual desire for Y that X believes that Y has specific features in virtue of which X desires Y. In both cases, the agent may be mistaken, or ignorant, as to why she feels herself attracted by another person. Again, the agent may feel either sexual desire, or the desire to love, without a specific object: She may urgently want to find an appropriate partner and fail in the search. Both sorts of desire can arise in the absence of a suitable object and remain unsatisfied for equally long periods of time. Both can be directed at an unsuitable object – unsuitable, that is, from the agent's point of view because she ranks the object low in her list of preferences.

These various kinds of similarities between love and sexual desire make it obvious that in the case of sexual desire we can draw a distinction parallel to that which we drew in the case of love. We can distinguish between sexually desiring – wishing to have sexually arousing bodily contact with – a particular person and sexually desiring anyone who possesses certain physical characteristics. All the questions that arise concerning exactly what it is that the agent loves in the partner arise also in connection with sexual desire. Does the agent desire bodily contact with anyone who has specific kinds of physical features – for example, a tawny skin, black hair, and a small waist – and desire contact only so long as they are present? Or does the agent find these characteristics to be sexually stimulating only in Mini? If the latter, what contribution, if any, do the rest of her physical features make to this stimulation? And what makes Mini's embodiment of these features so especially desirable?

To raise these questions is to draw attention to the need for making distinctions when the answers are given. Thus there certainly are situations in which people desire bodily contact only with partners who have specific kinds of physical features: Patrons of brothels are one familiar example of such people. Prostitutes who lose these specific features with age find it difficult to obtain work and are replaced by younger women who still have them. On the other hand, a doting husband or wife may find specific features to be sexually stimulating only in their spouses. The question why this should be so obviously has no general answer since the basis of their appeal lies in the psychological history of the particular agent. Sometimes other physical features make a contribution to this appeal and sometimes not. A woman still powerfully drawn to men who resemble her father in appearance may find that although a cleft chin is not essential in the men she loves, it adds to the appeal of those features, such as grey eyes and thin lips, that she does find essential. To ask why she finds these features to be required, and yet stimulating only in her spouse, may be to ask what sort of parental model she has internalized and what sort she has rejected. It is certainly to ask about her psychosexual needs and fears, her self-conception, and the conditions under which she feels secure in expressing deep emotion. Since we seldom have enough information about a particular person

63

to frame these questions in detail, we are seldom in a position to answer them properly.

Here we can draw a parallel with the case of love. It is possible, and perhaps likely, that the agent sometimes finds an entire person to be sexually desirable – not merely the person's entire body – and then discovers in him or her some physical features that the agent especially likes and picks out as the stimulant for his or her sexual desire. Given this situation, it will be Mini's sexual desire for Max, whatever condition his body happens to be in, that will lead her to believe, rightly or wrongly, that he instantiates certain physical properties in a uniquely desirable way. Yet if Mini can find Max to be sexually desirable despite the changes in his physical attributes, what is it, then, that she finds appealing? And is that different from the person, Max, for whom she sometimes has feelings of love?

Clearly, we must distinguish, both in the case of sexual desire and that of love, between the earlier and later stages of a relationship. If Mini feels sexual desire for Max when she is only slightly acquainted with him, the situation, and hence our description of it, will be very different from that of Mini's sexual desire for Max after they know each other intimately. In the first stage Mini may simply feel desire for what she takes to be a good representative of a type to which she is always drawn. Any presentable specimen of that physical type would elicit from her much the same sexual response. Since she knows Max so little, what she finds attractive can be only those physical qualities that he shares with other members of his type. As she comes to know him better and recognizes physical features that are distinctive of him, she may or may not find them sexually appealing. If she does, it may well be the case that they replace, in part, those of his class characteristics that she finds physically attractive about him. But by this time she will usually know something of him as a person also, and his sexual attractiveness will no longer be isolated from his psychological appeal.

64

The two will interact in such complex ways that what she finds physically appealing about him will no longer be simply a set of physical characteristics. Because these will embody his personality and character, Mini's sexual desire for him will be modified by the history of her personal relationship with him. What creates, or stimulates, her sexual desire will then be not his distinctive physical features alone but the manner in which they disclose the character of the man, Max, for whom she feels affection. Although his physical attributes will alter over time, they will continue to disclose, and be influenced by, his character and its changes. What Mini will continue to find sexually attractive about Max, if she does, will be the joint result of their life together: namely, the embodied character of Max.

3

Identifying the presence of love

It is commonly said that loving care for another person requires the lover to try to further the welfare and good of the beloved. To love someone is to will that person's good. The lover must try, in Tov-Ruach's words, 'to discover what the beloved is really like to determine the best development and exercise of the person's central features'. A lover, she goes on to say, whose 'attentions are active in forming and crystallizing the beloved's personality . . . takes care that his constituting attention is appropriate to the real traits and the tonal character of the person whom he loves'. (1980, p. 469) The question is how to interpret and then apply this precept.

In Colette's novel *Chéri*, for example, Léa, who is twice as old as Chéri, parts from him with the words:

You are breaking away from me very late in the day, my naughty little boy; I've been carrying you next to my heart for too long, and now you have a load of your own to carry: a young wife, perhaps a child . . . I am to blame for everything you lack . . . Yes, yes, my pretty, you are, thanks to me, at twenty-five, so light-hearted, so spoilt, and at the same time so sad . . . I'm very worried about you. You're going to suffer and make others suffer. You who have loved me . . . (1955, p. 166)

Here Léa is remarking that she has helped to create in Chéri someone who is inadequate to deal with his own future needs. Her attention has been active in forming his personality, and she certainly knows what he is really like. But has her 'constituting attention' been appropriate to the 'real traits and the tonal character' of Chéri? Are his 'real traits' and 'central

66

features' those inadequate ones that he now possesses? Or does he still have real traits that have been partly spoilt by Léa? It is far from clear how, in such a case, the real traits of the beloved are to be distinguished from those imposed or projected upon him by the lover. Yet it is this sort of case – one in which the lover has actively helped to form the personality of the beloved – that Tov-Ruach has chosen to illustrate the need for the lover's attention to be 'appropriate to the real traits and tonal character' of the beloved.

There is a further and related difficulty in Tov-Ruach's claim. It is that the beloved's 'real traits' and 'central features' are subject to change, not only by the lover's attentions but also by the development of other aspects of the personality of the beloved. In consequence, there is always a question, at any given time, as to which real traits require encouragement by the lover in order for them to develop and which traits do not. This is a separate question from that of which real traits the lover morally should, or should not, encourage. For many people have central traits that are far from admirable: selfishness, greediness, cruelty, for instance. These and various forms of infantilism and neuroticism may be embedded deeply in their personalities. Yet, as we know, such people can attract lovers who admire these traits under a different description, lovers who need to be dominated by aggressive and self-sufficient men or who need partners capable of expressing their own forbidden wishes. Sometimes these lovers know quite well what their beloved are 'really like' and try to arrange conditions for the 'best development and exercise' of the admired but morally worthless traits. There seems to be no reason why, on Tov-Ruach's account, love of this kind is not both genuine and appropriate. However, if this is so, then the lover's cultivation of the central features of the beloved may conflict with that person's moral welfare. The lover's concern with the partner's welfare may prevent the beloved from cultivating his or her real traits, and conversely. But can someone who loves genuinely and appropriately neglect either the moral welfare or the central traits of the beloved? If not, how are these two aspects of love supposed to be related to each other when they can so obviously come into conflict?

HOMOSEXUALITY AS A CENTRAL TRAIT

Clearly, the identification of the real character – the central traits – of the beloved will be, on Tov-Ruach's account, the lover's basic task; without it the lover will lack the understanding that creates appropriate love. Suppose then, that as a result of his efforts a man comes to realize that some of the central traits of his beloved are infantile or are neurotically based but that, nevertheless, he finds them attractive. Should he encourage them because they are basic features of the character of the loved person? Or should he withdraw his love because he believes that they produce unresolvable problems, moral or psychological, in the life of the beloved? Consider, then, some of the difficulties raised for Tov-Ruach's view by the case of male homosexuals who, according to psychoanalytic theory, suffer from strong castration fears. Most homosexual men, writes Otto Fenichel,

continue to be attracted by women, but, not being able to endure the idea of beings without a penis, they long for phallic women, for hermaphrodites, so to speak. This acute longing for objects with a penis compels them to choose boys, but the boys must have a maximum of girlish and feminine traits . . . and the homosexual ideal of the 'page boy' proves that they are actually looking for the 'girl with a penis'. (1946, p. 331)

Because this type of homosexual male, Fenichel says, identifies himself with his mother, he treats the youth who represent his adolescent self as he had wanted his mother to treat him. He gives to them 'the tenderness he had desired from his mother. While he acts as if he were his mother, emotionally he is centered in his love object, and thus enjoys being loved by himself'. (1946, p. 332)

Now if at least some homosexual men can be described accurately in this way, then strong castration fears and developed narcissism are basic traits in their personalities. These traits can produce behaviour – a form of self-sufficiency, for example – that is attractive to some people. Yet when characterized psychoanalytically in this way, the traits in themselves are neither attractive to anyone nor morally admirable. Their attractiveness depends either upon their being characterized differently or upon their being interpreted as tolerable elements in a personality whose other features make it attractive. In either case, it is not clear how to apply the injunction that the lover's attention be directed at determining 'the conditions for the best development and exercise of the person's central features'. Is the lover to believe that such traits are not of central importance in the character of the beloved? This is hardly plausible when anything so far-reaching in a person's life as his or her sexual role is at issue. Is the devoted lover to reject the psychoanalytic characterization, as many homosexuals do, on the ground that it is simply mistaken? To do this requires the lover to give reasons why the characterization is mistaken when applied to homosexual men in general or to one of them in particular.

Thus the problem for the lover is to give an account of the basic traits of the beloved that will explain why the latter is homosexual rather than heterosexual. If the account does not do this, then the lover will lack the understanding that enables him to love a homosexual man appropriately. The lover will also lack the same sort of understanding of himself. But of course these are very difficult conditions to meet. They demand that the lover achieve a level of self-knowledge and understanding denied to most people, homosexual and heterosexual alike. Any injunction that is so difficult to put into practice as that of Tov-Ruach may be a moral imperative, but it cannot be a description of ordinary examples of 'appropriate love'.

However, someone might try to defend Tov-Ruach by

arguing that homosexual (or lesbian) love is by its very nature inappropriate because it is based on misconceptions, or perhaps self-deception, concerning the character of the beloved. The homosexual, it might be urged, is not his own mother and should not identify himself with her. Nor should he treat his youthful beloved as his own adolescent self had wanted to be treated by his mother. Misidentification, and its consequent narcissism, are the outcome of false belief and misunderstanding: The homosexual lover's actual relationship to his beloved is quite different from what he takes, and sometimes pretends, it to be. In this respect it must be inappropriate. Given this fact, there is no possibility of the homosexual carrying out Tov-Ruach's injunction that the genuine lover should try to discover the conditions under which the beloved's real character can develop best. For there is no possibility in a homosexual relationship of the lover discovering the real character, the central traits, of the beloved. While similar sorts of misconceptions arise in the case of heterosexual love – Fenichel instances narcissistic men who love boyish girls as 'the feminine parts of their own ego (p. 333) – these misconceptions, contrary to those of homosexual love, are not necessary elements in love between men and women. Thus Tov-Ruach's injunction fits well with the psychoanalytic account of homosexuality and perverted heterosexuality. But when the psychoanalytic account itself is rejected and not replaced by some other account that also enables us to identify basic traits, Tov-Ruach's injunction becomes inapplicable. Its utility depends upon our being able to identify 'central features'. Yet its author does not give us the information necessary for us to do this.

LOVING AND BEING IN LOVE

Often a distinction is made between loving someone and being in love with someone, although the basis of the distinction tends to remain obscure. We love many people, objects, animals, and situations; but we are in love with very few of them, and usually they are people. In what, then, does the difference consist? 'Being in love', writes Hunter, 'is not a definable set of emotional qualities'. If John tells Mary that he has tender feelings toward her, and then says that

> he thinks of her night and day . . . dotes on her every gesture and so on, he would still, no matter how long the catalogue might be, have stopped short of saying that he was in love. Nor does Mary, if she is a normal human being, know what the list should include. There is no point at which she could say, 'That's enough. You are in love'. (1983, pp. 70–1)

In brief, Hunter says being in love is not something that we can discover by self-scrutiny of our behaviour. It is something that we learn by realizing that we are willing to meet, and to sanction, certain expectations. These are 'to give ungrudgingly, and to treat the loved one's interests as if they were our own' because of our enthusiasm for, and readiness to unite ourselves with, that person, doing this 'in such a way that the joint interest is primary' and other people are excluded. (pp. 75–6) Thus, according to Hunter, being in love is a matter of being willing, because of enthusiasm for the beloved, to make our united interests primary. This commonly, although not invariably, requires a willingness to live together. (p. 74)

But is this the best way to describe the crucial differences between being in love with someone and simply loving that person? That some sort of enthusiasm, and the wish to make their united interests primary, are necessary conditions of people being in love with each other is not really in dispute; without these conditions there would be no grounds for anyone to assert that the agent was in love rather than in some other state such as attentiveness, sympathy, or solicitude. On the other hand, a mother and her adult daughter who operate a business together can be enthusiastic in some ways toward each other and have their united interests primary, in some sense, without being in love with anyone except their respective husbands. Toward their own husbands, mother and daughter may each feel enthusiastic, and each may wish to unite her interests with those of her husband because she is in love with him. There is a difference, therefore, between these two sets of relationships, that of mother–daughter and wife–husband, a difference that is not explained by the presence of unanalyzed enthusiasm and the mere union of interests.

Let us consider the difference between discovering that we love a particular person and discovering that we are in love with a particular person. It is of the latter that Hunter claims self-examination to be useless. Instead, the lover has to agree to fulfill commitments of enthusiasm and to make union of interests primary. Now if, as Hunter says, being in love 'is not a definable set of emotional qualities', what is the status of enthusiasm? surely it is at least a necessary ingredient of love? If enthusiasm is not an emotional quality – if it is not closely related to passion, devotion, zeal, ardour, fervour, eagerness, and warmth – what is it? Can we be in love unenthusiastically? Are there genuine lovers who are genuinely cold toward each other, experience no feelings, undergo no physical agitation? Clearly not. In addition, there is the question how we learn, or know, that we are willing to fulfill the expectation of united interests. Surely we do not have to announce our willingness publicly in order to discover that we have it? True, this may happen on occasion and catch us by surprise either in its existence or in its timing. The latter is perhaps the more common since the occasion on which a partially formed resolution will become public is often not anticipated. The last scene between Will and Dorothea in George Eliot's *Middlemarch*, for example, is of a consequence foreseen by neither:

At last he turned, still resting against the chair, and stretching his hand automatically toward his hat, said with a sort of exasperation, 'Good-bye'.

'Oh, I cannot bear it – my heart will break', said Dorothea, starting from her seat, the flood of her young passion bearing down all the obstructions which had kept her silent – the great tears rising and falling in an instant: 'I don't mind about poverty – I hate my wealth'.

In an instant Will was close to her and had his arms round her, but she drew her head back and held his away gently that she might go on speaking, her large tear-filled eyes looking at his very simply, while she said in a sobbing childlike way, 'We could live quite well on my own fortune – it is too much – seven hundred a year – I want so little – no new clothes – and I will learn what everything costs'. (1965, p. 870)

Ordinarily, however, we realize, before we announce it to anyone else, that we are willing to unite our interests with those of our beloved. We come to this realization, in part, by asking ourselves, and then deciding, whether this is the sort of arrangement that we can and wish to have with our partner. This is not self-observation, but it is self-interrogation, and certainly one form of self-examination since we are in the process of working out our answer to the question, What is to be done? Similarly, we can ask ourselves what kind and degree of enthusiasm we feel for our partner, and we can obtain a useful answer. In both cases, self-interrogation is one way of making explicit to ourselves that we are, or are not, in love with a given person. If we do not ask ourselves the question we may never consider the answer. Sometimes, especially if we are ignorant and inexperienced, we discover that the pattern of actions, thoughts, and feelings – a pattern already recognized by us as a pattern – is to be characterized in a way, that of being in love, that had not occurred to us previously. There are many reasons why it may not have occurred to us, but a reason common in cases of first love is our mere lack of knowledge that our pattern of behaviour is one form that love takes. Hence it is not at all odd to ask of someone who has observed us closely, 'Do you really think that I am in love?'. By contrast, we sometimes come to realize that our behaviour, thoughts, and feelings, when considered together for the first time, exemplify a pattern known to us as being in love; and we also realize that even though we had been unaware of the presence of this pattern previously, there is no doubt now of its existence: We are in love.

THE GROUNDS FOR CLAIMING TO BE IN LOVE

It is possible, under certain conditions, for someone to become aware of the pattern of his or her behaviour, or of its proper characterization, while still being mistaken as to which person is the beloved. For instance, a man may feel affection amounting to love for two sisters, Ann and Annette, but be unable honestly to decide which he would prefer to live with, and then in some new and testing situation – her departure for example – find himself drawn to Ann by such longing that he suddenly realizes how for some time past it had been quiet Ann to whom he had been deeply attached rather than the lively Annette by whom he had been dazzled. In such a case the test has not forced him to decide which person he prefers; it has revealed to him which person he already prefers. If it is objected that in the circumstances described no test could make this distinction, then the objector is assuming that the lover's recognition of his own state will in itself ensure that he knows what he wants – that he thereby knows the object of his love. But this is not true, for he can come to recognize his pattern of behaviour, or come to characterize it, as love and yet find that the pattern seems to center on two people, Ann and Annette, equally. He then mistakenly believes that he is in love with both of them; and he also mistakenly believes that it is impossible for him to decide which of them he loves the more. The effect of Ann's departure is to reveal to him the unsuspected intensity of his feeling for her, an intensity that was not apparent to him as long as she was so closely associated with her sister that he did not distinguish his feelings for one from his feelings for the other.

74

Now recognizing a pattern of behaviour and giving it a name can be aided by the agent asking himself or herself or telling other people, what beliefs, desires, and feelings he or she has concerning the person in question. So when a woman tells her beloved that she thinks of him night and day, that she dotes on his every gesture, she is providing him with useful, though not clinching, evidence that she is in love with him. It is useful because thinking about him constantly, being delighted by his presence, and pained by his absence are characteristic of being in love. They usually precede, and then accompany, a profession of love. If they were absent from someone who claimed to be in love, we should seriously question the strength of the agent's desire since it would manifest itself only in the words that professed the love. But in the absence of supporting evidence – actions, reports of daydreams, signs of pleasure – we should wonder whether the desire amounted to anything more than a readiness to follow a convention of appropriate response.

We should have the same doubt if the profession of love itself were so conventionally phrased as to seem perfunctory. Thus at one point in Theodor Fontane's novel *Effi Briest* the engaged girl, Effi, discusses her forthcoming marriage:

'I'm . . . well, I'm all in favour of equality. Love and tenderness of course, as well. But if you can't achieve love and tenderness because love, according to papa, is nonsense anyway (though I don't believe it) well, then I'm in favour of wealth and a splendid house – a really splendid one where royal princes come to shoot or where the old Emperor drives up and has a gracious word for all the ladies – even the young ones. And when eventually we move to Berlin, then I'm in favour of court balls and gala performances at the opera with a seat somewhere in the royal box'.
'Are you putting all this forward as a joke, out of high spirits?'
'No, Mama, I'm absolutely serious. Love comes first, but immediately afterwards comes luxury and a position in society; and after that comes entertainment – yes, entertainment. Always something new, something that will make me laugh or cry. The one thing I can't stand is boredom'. (1962, pp. 17–8)

Love or marriage, or both, are traditionally a prophylactic for boredom, but when they are entered into chiefly for that reason, both their genuineness and efficacy disappear.

However, even good supporting evidence of a nonverbal kind is not clinching. It is compatible with states other than that of being in love – for example, with feeling great affection for, and hence loving, but not being in love with, a particular person. Loving someone often reveals itself in many of the same ways as does being in love: in thinking about, and doting upon, the person; in delight at the person's presence; in the desire to further the person's welfare; in the uniting of interests; and in the readiness to feel pain and anger at being frustrated in those common interests. Because we cannot be in love with someone without also loving that person, we can sometimes be uncertain as to which state is present on a given occasion.

The most obvious, but not infallible, sign of Max being in love with Mini, as distinct from merely loving her, is his intense desire to be inseparable from her, to unite his daily activities with hers rather than merely uniting their interests. Max can love Mini, or love some of her aspects, without wishing to be with her constantly, for he may fear the guilt and anxiety that an intimate relationship would create in him. But he cannot be in love with her and yet not prefer, or at least wish, that the situation were otherwise – wish that their lives, and hence their activities and interests, were inseparable, that many of their most intimate activities were pursued together. However, the desire to be inseparable is not a sufficient condition of being in love since if Max were deranged he might wish to unite all his activities with Mini's; and if she were similarly afflicted she might wish the same. But their union on that basis alone would not be one of love: It might be that of reciprocal mistrust. Furthermore, while a disastrous relationship can be renounced although the people concerned still love each other, they may well no longer be in love with each other. They will not be if they have renounced their desire to be inseparable, their desire to possess an important part of each other's lives, rather than merely renouncing the enactment of their desires. It is for this reason that the most helpful answer to the question 'How can I tell whether I am in love with her?' is simply 'By agreeing that you are prepared to share the most intimate and important parts of your life with her'. Thus Coleridge's characterization of love as 'a desire of the whole being to be united to something, or some being, felt necessary to its completeness' is really a characterization of either the state of being in love with someone or of the wish to find someone with whom to be in love. It is not a characteristic of love in the sense of mere tender concern or affection.

FALLING IN LOVE

People are said to fall in and out of love as they are not said to fall in and out of anger, fear, jealousy, hate, shame, joy, remorse, and many of the other emotions. Why is this? It cannot be that the onset, or the termination, of being in love is more sudden than that of joy or fear or anger, for that is obviously not true. A pang of fear, jealousy, or joy is as sudden as falling head over heels in love. The explanation of this difference in the case of love seems to lie not in the varying intensity of feeling that we display in different emotions, for we can be possessed by most of them to a greater or less degree, but in the small role that any given belief need play both in love and in the process of falling in love. The latter resembles the onset of sexual desire and hunger in not requiring the agent to hold any specific beliefs about the person or thing except that he or she or it is a fitting object of the agent's desire. The agent's readiness to respond to such an object produces a dispositional pattern of behaviour in which the agent's other beliefs about the object of desire are substantially inoperative in that they do not affect his or her desire. The agent becomes a patient, and is overcome by desire for the object: that is, does not critically examine, and intervene in, the process of seeking it. The process is nonrational.

Emotional turmoil is also present, of course, in states of rage, gloom, and some forms of error. In such states the agent commonly becomes a patient through succumbing to the temptations presented by strong desires and specifiable beliefs. But in the case of love, sexual desire, and hunger the agent does so because strong desires need not be controlled by any particular beliefs about the object. In other states such as certain kinds of rage, error, and gloom – those nonphysiologically induced – that depend largely on specifiable beliefs, the agent makes mistakes, or loses control to desire, because of particular beliefs about the object or situation. A woman believes that her child has been hurt or that her mother has died or that her guilt is clear. When these beliefs are altered, by whatever means, the state disappears: Her guilt-ridden gloom is replaced by equanimity, error by knowledge, rage by calm. No such alteration of beliefs need have similar results in the case of love, sexual desire, and hunger, except that the object may prove to be incapable of satisfying the desire. The desire or attraction may remain although unsatisfied: Hunger need not disappear simply because the intended food turns out to be inedible; nor need the disposition to fall in love disappear simply because the intended partner turns out to be unavailable.

We must distinguish, then, between the nonrational process of falling in love with someone and the process, which may be thoughtful and well considered, of coming to love a person. Similarly, we need to distinguish between the nonrational process of falling out of love with a particular person, and the process, often reason-guided, of ceasing to love a particular person. The reasons why a person falls out of love with someone are usually no clearer to the agent than the reasons why he or she fell in love. In both cases, of course, the agent commonly attempts to give reasons, but since the original process was not rationally guided, neither is its reversal likely to be. The unconscious needs and wishes that produced the original love usually remain unconscious when it is abandoned; and the agent's disappointment and frustration at finding his or her needs and wishes unfulfilled – or fantasies unrealized – seek expression in justificatory accounts that make no mention of the forces actually at work. If the agent were able to mention such forces, then either the agent would have learned, while in love, something about his or her previously unconscious needs and wishes, or would never have fallen in love with – as distinct from coming to love – the beloved in the first place.

Falling in love overlaps with infatuation but they are not identical notions. For, as we have already suggested, there is weak-willed infatuation in addition to that of blind desire – desire that expresses unconscious needs and wishes – and it is only the latter that operates in the case of falling in love. There is also heedless or reckless infatuation, and this is distinct from falling in love. Someone who becomes infatuated with some activity through weakness of will, or through recklessness, while aware of the weighty considerations that tell against the course of action, is irrational in not allowing himself or herself to be guided by reason. This is not, however, a case of falling in love, for people do not fall in love with someone through weakness of will or recklessness but through desire. A man or woman may fall in love under circumstances in which, given their ages, positions, and goals, it is natural, socially expected, and psychologically satisfactory that they be swept away by blind desire for the beloved, while displaying neither recklessness nor weakness of will. Yet a man who falls in love by being overcome by desire may nevertheless select well in two respects: first, in not holding important false beliefs about the character of the beloved, and second, in believing correctly that his character and that of his beloved will form a satisfactory partnership. By hypothesis, the procedure of selection will be rationally weak, but despite that the result may be adequate.

Hence the agent swept away by desire is nonrational to the extent that considerations pro and con do not arise for the agent any more than they do in the case of a hungry woman confronted with what seems to be satisfactory food. She does not ask herself whether she has good reasons for eating it, and such considerations do not guide her. Now falling in love is sometimes a case of blind infatuation – that is, love based on unconscious wishes and desires. But the infatuation due to recklessness or weakness of will is guided by bad reasons, whereas the infatuation of falling in love is guided by no reasons. For in recklessness there are displayed the agent's poor judgments and evaluations, employed as reasons, concerning the nature and consequences of his actions. In weakness of will there is conscious inability to conform to the requirements of known good reasons; but in blind desire there is suspension of guidance by reasons, whether good or bad.

The eventual outcome of falling in love with a particular person may be either being in love with, and hence loving, the person, or it may be simply loving him or her. Many people never fall in love: That is, they are never overwhelmed by a desire for an inseparable union of daily and intimate activities with their beloved. They never undergo what is the psychological equivalent of physiological sexual desire. On the other hand, these people, having come by other means to love their partners, may be in love with them as much as, or more than, those people who came together by falling in love. How we came to be in love is a very different question from that of whether we are in love with, or simply love, one another. Similarly, our professing that we love a particular person can have very different implications and consequences from our professing that we are in love with that person. The former is much more various in the types of its objects, and in the degrees of intensity with which they are

80

cherished, than the latter. Since being in love with someone is only one of many forms of love, professing it has a more easily specifiable range of implications and consequences than a simple profession of love. A woman who professes to be in love with a man can reasonably be taken as suggesting that she would like to live with him, if conditions permit, and to share his life. But a woman who professes to love a man may be referring to her son or brother or father, and living with him, or sharing most of the intimate areas of his life, may be an unwelcome suggestion. She may simply admire and value him as a trustworthy kinsman. This socially approved relationship would become a very different one if the woman suddenly announced that she was in love with one of these men and was guilty of incest.

BEING IN LOVE: BELIEFS AND DECISIONS

To claim that no particular belief held by someone need have any bearing, or effect, on his or her love is certainly not to claim that all the agent's beliefs are irrelevant to it. For when people fall out of love they commonly do so, in part, because of a change in their beliefs: They discover unpleasant alterations in their partner's characters, or decide that the relationship was based on mistaken beliefs about each other, or find that their beliefs about their own needs and desires have changed. In consequence, their feelings, desires, and evaluations also change. To the extent that these altered beliefs affect the partners' desires, feelings, and preferences, the relationship between the partners will be changed by their new beliefs. Of course, falling out of love – as with falling in love – may occur without the intermediary of changed beliefs. It may take place through mere loss of the desire to be inseparable from the partner, and while the agent may be able to give reasons for this loss of desire, they may be reasons of preference alone and be phrased in terms of boredom or satiation or moral revulsion in which alteration of belief, as distinct from evaluation plays no overt part.

In the first volume of his autobiography Bertrand Russell remarks: 'I went out bicycling one afternoon, and suddenly, as I was riding along a country road, I realized that I no longer loved Alys. I had no idea until this moment that my love for her was even lessening'. Russell then says that in part his feelings toward Alys had changed because he had come to see in her some of the features that he strongly disliked in her mother and brothers: self-righteousness, insincerity, malice, deceitfulness. 'During my bicycle ride a host of such things occurred to me, and I became aware that she was not the saint I had always supposed her to be'. (1967, pp. 147–8) This sudden awareness of a change of feeling is characteristic of both falling in and out of love. In both cases there may be no alteration in the beliefs held by the agent concerning his or her partner. At the other extreme is separation based entirely on the presence of only one new belief: that in the partner's unfaithfulness.

Perhaps the most important belief that people hold in relationships of love is the belief that a relationship of this kind exists between them. This is especially important when two people claim to be in love with each other, for then the mere loss of this belief by one partner may, and often does, lead to its loss by the other. This effect can be produced in many ways, for the belief that we are no longer loved by a partner commonly affects our capacity and desire to continue to love the partner. Our prospects are changed and we have to decide what attitude to take toward them – to decide whether our prospects are so altered that our commitment to the relationship should be withdrawn. The decision is complicated by the fact that we can be mistaken in believing that we were or are in love with our partner, and hence can also be mistaken in believing that we are no longer in love with that person. We can believe falsely that we no longer have enough affection for our partner to wish, any longer, to make our united interests primary. We can discover our mistake by finding, when put to the test in action, that we still do wish to join our interests in this way; and we may infer, correctly, that the reason we do so is not because of habit or pity or fear of change but because of continued affection. Similarly, we may hold the false belief that we do not love someone, our father, for example, but discover after his final illness that we were deeply attached to him.

How do these mistakes arise, and how do we discover them? They arise because both loving someone and being in love with someone are complex and variable patterns of behavioural dispositions and episodes, feelings, and thoughts. To recognize that a particular relationship exemplifies such a pattern requires more than the agent's willingness to assert that it does. Nor is it sufficient that the agent be willing to commit himself or herself to fulfilling certain sorts of expectations held by the partner. The agent's assertion can be, and sometimes is, wrong in fact; and the agent's pledge to meet the partner's expectations, although reliable, may be motivated by considerations other than love — duty, for example, or the desire for useful action. Because the agent can be mistaken about his or her motives, the agent can equally well be mistaken about the nature of the behavioural pattern in which they are, and will be, embedded. For this reason, among others, it is not necessary that an agent who loves someone believe that he or she does so. The agent may love the person, as shown by actions, attitudes, and thoughts, while never having given the matter any explicit consideration. The agent may also, of course, have considered the matter and given the wrong answer.

The two common reasons for giving the wrong answer to the question 'Am I in love with her?' are, as we saw earlier, nonrecognition of the existence of a pattern and mislabelling of a pattern known to exist. The latter confusion is possible because the agent, through inattention, faulty memory, or repression, often does not notice the differences between the course of his activities and that of some related pattern such as friendship or benevolence. The former mistake – that of nonrecognition – commonly arises from lack of information due, again, to inattention, inexperience, or repression: The agent does not realize that over a period of time his actions have displayed a family resemblance to each other, that he has been preoccupied with the same set of topics, and that other people can accurately predict his responses concerned with his partner even when he himself cannot.

There is, however, a third source of error. It arises from the agent's combined lack of knowledge and lack of decision about the future. If, when her pattern of behaviour is still being developed, a woman asks herself whether she loves a particular person, her answer must be uncertain and can easily be incorrect. She is asking herself not only to categorize a number of her actions, thoughts, and feelings, past and present, but also to predict the course of their future development. Yet their course will depend, in part, on decisions that she has still to make, decisions that, if they are to be genuine at the time, the woman cannot now make in the guise of forecasting the future.

Hence a woman, in answering 'I don't know' to the question 'Are you in love with him?' is often saying that she does not know what decisions bearing on this matter she will make in the future. Part of the information that she lacks is knowledge of what judgments she will come to make concerning him: whether she will decide that the two of them have sufficient interests in common for her to seek his regular company; whether she will decide that his temperament will please her in the long term; whether she will decide that her affection for him is sufficient for her to confide in him; or whether she will decide, finally, that they wish to share each other's lives. It is true that these decisions, in turn, will be likely to depend, in part, on future information about her partner and herself – likely but not necessarily. For on any one of these issues it is possible that no new information will come to hand, and that if a decision is to be made the agent will have to use information already available to her. At some point she may well be forced to make a decision about what the future character of the relationship is to be, whether it is to be mere friendship or something else, whether it is to be encouraged or terminated. So no matter how much information she accumulates, she is likely at some later time to have to make a judgment that concerns her future prospects and living arrangements. If asked at that time whether she loves, or is in love with, him the agent's answer will record her decision and not merely her observation of her own state of mind.

Such cases are to be distinguished from those in which the agent reflects on the relationship and comes to realize that in a sense the answer has already been settled by the existence of a pattern, that no decision is required since earlier actions and behaviour have already made it unnecessary. In short, the agent's answer can be either backward-looking or forward-looking, and the grounds of the agent's answer will vary accordingly. If the agent is not aware of this difference she is likely to treat the question 'Am I in love with him?' as a simple request for information about her psychological attitude toward him. She may believe that simply by scanning the evidence she ought to be able to give either an affirmative or negative answer – or at least an uncertain one that simply expresses the agent's incomplete evidence, for the question does not usually arise until the relationship seems to make the question an appropriate one.

BEING IN LOVE: THE STRENGTH OF A DISPOSITION

Sometimes, then, the question 'Am I in love with him?' is answered as though it asked whether a particular episode were occurring. The question 'Do I feel a pang of love?' is taken to resemble 'Do I feel a heart-throb?' – questions whose answers are to be given by introspection of certain bodily sen-

85

sations or certain states of mind. Sometimes, however, the question is interpreted as requesting information about a process that is thought of as carrying along the agent, like flotsam on a flood tide, independently of his or her efforts and wishes. Loving, or being in love with, someone is treated as though it were always like falling in love, as though loving a person simply consisted in the agent being overwhelmed by desire for the company of the beloved and being swept on to some final phase. The agent is asked to note whether he or she is in the grip of such a force and to report accordingly. The model is that of the display of a propensity such as avarice, pride, humility, or boredom. In order to answer the query concerning love, the agent is supposed by self-examination to report both on episodes of affectionate thought or behaviour and on the propensity that they express. Just as a person can display isolated instances of avarice, pride, or humility toward someone else without having a general disposition to be avaricious, proud, or humble toward that or any other person, so someone can display isolated instances of loving behaviour toward a person without having a general disposition to love him or her. The question, Are you – or are you not – in love with him? can be used to ask either whether the episodes are isolated instances or whether a disposition is thought to be present.

Nevertheless, this question is obviously incomplete. The point of asking it is usually a practical one: The inquirer wishes to know what action or course of behaviour the agent is prepared, or likely, to take because of affection for the beloved. It is true that merely to know that the agent loves someone may be, in principle, of interest to the questioner even though circumstances are such that nothing much can occur as a result of that love. The interest of this sort of case, however, is commonly that of speculating about what might have occurred if conditions had been different – if the agent's love had been expressed in some significant way in behaviour or had made a difference to other people's lives. The interest of the more usual case is that of knowing what is likely to happen next, and for that purpose the inquirer needs to know how much the agent loves the person, how much he or she is willing to do in consequence of that love. The question to be asked is 'How much am I – or are you – in love with M?' Are you, for example, prepared to assume responsibility for M's well-being? Are you willing to have M live with you? Is M to be a beneficiary in your will? Who will look after M if you die? These are characteristic questions for which answers are desired when we ask about one person's love for another, and thus about the strength of that love. Actions speak louder than words in such cases because it is actions, usually future actions, in which we have an interest when framing this sort of question.

Hence when the agent says, 'I do not know whether I am in love with M', the agent is usually saying that he does not know how much he or she loves M, whether it is enough for adoption or marriage, or too much for trifling with M's affections. This is because it is easier for us to discern the presence of some affection, either in ourselves or in other people, than it is to know its real strength. The latter is revealed to us only when put to the test of crucial actions; the former, by contrast, makes itself plain in the common interchange of daily behaviour. That Max obviously seeks the company of Mini, that only he laughs at her indifferent jokes, that he goes out of his way to favour her at work, that he seizes the opportunity to perform unnecessary services on her behalf – these, when taken together, are typical and clear signs of affection. How much affection they indicate is less clear. Would Max give up his job in order to follow her elsewhere? Would he sacrifice his leisure time in order that she could attend a training course? Would he marry her even though he would then have to support her aged parents on his small salary? The possible tests are innumerable, but most of them may never arise, and perhaps never will until actually needed for answering, in a practical situation, the question 'How much does Max love Mini?'

In this way affection resembles other capabilities such as physical strength. That our legs have some strength we know from daily experience. But how much they have we can find out only by subjecting them to unusual strain. Commonly, this is also the way in which we discover the strength of our love for someone: We either imagine, or are actually placed in, testing circumstances, and we use the answers drawn from these tests as our stock of information. Sometimes, of course, we assert that no such tests are needed because the strength of our love will pass any test; we have committed our affections completely and irrevocably. But whether this is so can only be determined by testing the strength of our commitment, by treating it as a pledge that needs to be carried out in suitable action.

THE STRENGTH AND IDENTIFY OF MOMENTARY FEELINGS

Clearly, we can test the strength of a propensity by its consequences in action. What, though, of a pang of love or of a 'momentary feeling of love?' If we can identify a pang or momentary feeling as one of love, how do we determine its strength? Are there variations of intensity that we somehow recognize although they have no effect in our actions? And can we mistake one sort of pang or momentary feeling for another sort – mistake a pang of contrition for one of affection? If so, I can be wrong in claiming that just now I felt a pang, or had a feeling of love for Mini, and I could have been justified in saying that I was uncertain.

There is no doubt that people do have pangs of love or throbs of pride or shocks of grief. These bodily sensations are identified by the different situations in which they arise, including the objects to which they are directed: the voice of the beloved, the graduation ceremony, the deathbed scene. Sometimes, however, the phrase 'momentary feeling' is not used to refer to a bodily sensation occurring in a certain context of behaviour. The phrase is used, instead, to refer to those short-lived hopes, fears, wishes, desires, joys, and other mental episodes that, having no obvious connection with the main lines of our activity, well up in us suddenly. Whereas the strength of a pang or throb or shock is simply the strength of a bodily sensation that can be faint or sharp, long or short, local or diffuse, isolated or repeated, the strength of short-lived or episodic thoughts is obviously different from that of sensations. A flutter in the stomach can be very pronounced, and so can a flutter of fear. But the intensity of strength of our fears need not be of the same sort as the strength of our flutters of fear. Although states of strong fear are accompanied by strong flutters, not all our fears are actual states of fear. Some of our fears are thoughts of unpleasant outcomes whose contemplation is merely disturbing but whose realization would be frightening. Moreover, many fearful thoughts of a momentary sort have no associated sensations. To say, 'For a moment I feared that she would be late', need not be claiming to have had an actual flutter of fear. We discover the strength of fearful thoughts by considering both the agent's description of them and the detailed circumstances in which they appear, including the presence of sensations and other physical symptoms. Now some momentary feelings – as distinct from mere bodily sensations – lead to spontaneous action, as when a man unexpectedly meets his estranged wife, and disarmed for the moment by memories of past affection, greets her with a tender kiss. If we know enough about these two people, their previous relationship, and the customs of their social group, we can judge the strength of the man's feeling as revealed in his action. The strength of his feeling explains the degree of seriousness of his action. The fact that, by hypothesis, his feeling of affection lasts only a short time does not alter the significance of his action, for we are assuming that the action was the unstudied expression of his thought and desire at that moment. If it was unstudied, then his feeling of affection was stronger than if he had been content merely to shake hands with his wife or nod to her or pass by without speaking. How much affection he felt was shown by his kiss. He was placed in an uncommon situation whose outcome he neither planned nor foresaw, and perhaps would not have believed possible beforehand. Of course he might have suppressed his feelings and passed by. But in that case his action was not unstudied.

Other momentary feelings, whether of joy, fear, hope, or desire, may be unaccompanied by bodily sensations and lead to no action, either because none is possible or because it is suppressed. Yet these feelings can vary in strength and intensity. The hope that comes to me when I mishear the reply, and for a moment mistakenly believe that I have been offered the job, can be modest or grandiose in the consequences that I envisage and the decisions I propose. The anger that I feel when I am misinformed that my qualifications have been rejected by the department is an anger that lasts only until correction is made; but that anger may be as intense as a more enduring one or as slight as any sign of mere irritation. This variation depends on the seriousness of what the agent would be prepared to do and think concerning the objects of these feelings – that which is feared or hoped for or regretted – if the agent were willing and able to express these feelings in behaviour. If I feel as though I should like to scream at the job interviewer, denounce him, and damage his office before slamming the door behind me, this description of my suppressed impulse indicates a much stronger momentary feeling of anger than if I accurately describe myself as simply wishing to say, 'I don't really want your job anyway'. Of course, I may misdescribe my momentary feeling or, for some reason, not be able to describe it; or two instances of a particular sort of feeling – joy for example – may be indistinguishable in strength because my descriptions of them, and the circumstances in which I have them, provide no basis for discriminating between their intensity.

The strength of brief feelings, then, sometimes accompanied by bodily sensations and other physical expressions, can be measured by the courses of action toward which they incline us – courses of action that may or may not be carried out. That is, their strength is judged, when this is possible, by the physical activity and voluntary actions to which they would lead if exhibited in behaviour. These actions can often be ranked by their degree of importance for the agent: that is, by the extent to which the agent believes that they would affect people's lives, including the agent's own. An angry impulse that results in the death of a person is believed to be more serious, in most societies, than one that produces only injured pride for a day. On the other hand, suppose that I have a momentary feeling of envy at the sight of my host's new piano, envy that takes the form either of my having a visual image of the piano placed in my own house or of my exclaiming to myself, 'That should be mine since I could make so much better use of it then he can'. Between these two expressions of envy there is nothing to choose as to degree of strength. For if they both were exhibited in behaviour their outcomes would be the same: The piano would become mine by unspecified means. But our information about the two instances is so meager that we cannot distinguish between them as to the degree of seriousness of their projected courses of action.

Similarly, we are not always well enough placed to be able to distinguish a pang of hope from a pang of contrition, a throb of joy from a throb of pride, or a momentary feeling of anger from one of hate. The reason why we sometimes mistake one for the other, and are open to later correction either by ourselves or by someone else, is that our understanding of our role in the situation, and of the situation itself, is defective for various reasons. Thus we can mistake our momentary admiration for affection, or momentary pride for benevolence, or jealousy for envy, because, for example, we have erroneous beliefs about our own motives and desires, and perhaps mistaken views, also, concerning the other participants and factors in the situation. We may believe, wrongly, that a person is soliciting our affection, and in a wish to reciprocate in some way, we interpret our flash of admiration of the person's abilities as one of affection for the person. That is, if asked, we should describe our momentary feeling as one of affection rather than admiration. Our mistake might be revealed by an examination of our motives, desires, and beliefs concerning the relationship between us, for it is from our understanding of that relationship that our momentary feeling arises.

It is a familiar point that the bodily sensations – the throbs, pangs, and flashes – that accompany these momentary desires and beliefs are of no help by themselves in distinguishing one momentary feeling from another: The sensations associated with different feelings may be of the same type, and different instances of the same sort of feeling may have different sensations. The physiological agitation of anger, and the accompanying sensations may, but need not, be different from the agitation and sensations of fear; the bodily pang of contrition can be indistinguishable as a sensation from the pang of hope. So the only way in which we can identify our momentary feelings is by the circumstances in which they arise and, in particular, by our evaluations and appraisals of the objects – or of the situations – to which they are directed. To make these identifications is often very difficult, and sometimes impossible, for us at the time when the feelings occur. We can, for instance, be subject to complex mixtures of responses: ashamed at having been publicly criticized, humbled before superior authority, and vexed at having failed in our project. If our powers of psychological analysis and observation, and our linguistic skills, are poor, then we shall not be successful in identifying the shame, humility, and chagrin that make up our complex response. But, as we have seen, even when our response is an unmixed one, we may fail to recognize it or may be uncertain of its nature. To know whether, at a given moment, we are feeling envy or jealousy, hate or anger, joy or pride, or some combination of these, demands not only that we be familiar with the distinctive features of these emotions but also that we be able to recognize the presence of these features in our brief responses. If we are handicapped by such defence mechanisms as emotional repression, displacement, projection, or reaction formation, we may not find it possible to recognize the appropriate features. Again, we may find it difficult or impossible to describe them in a way satisfactory to others, or perhaps to ourselves. We may, for example, not be able to decide which term to apply because we are ignorant of the cause and other circumstances of our emotion, or because we are confused as to what we think about the object of our emotion – the beloved, the hated, or the feared. One common reason for such confusion is lack of information, and hence uncertainty, concerning what reciprocal emotion is, or will be, directed at us by another agent in the relationship.

Thus mere physiological agitation in ourselves does not tell us whether we are experiencing an emotion or are displaying the symptoms of illness. This is why our grasp of our situation is commonly so important in our being able to identify the emotion that we are undergoing. If neither we nor anyone else understands our circumstances, then no one knows what emotion we are experiencing, or indeed whether we are simply ill or being subjected by someone else to physiological stimuli. It is true that infants experience fear without being able to judge that their situation is appropriate to that emotion. But the fact that the fright-response of infants does not have to be learned shows us that our adult appraisal of situations as fearful has a genetic prototype. Infants do not judge, but they are born with what are, in effect, ready-made mechanisms of appraisal: Their fear-response is produced only by their bodily recognition of specific kinds of stimuli as 'fearful' ones.

93

4

Emotions and attitudes: Loving a person

It is a striking feature of our terms for the emotions that many of the same terms are also used for character traits, for the virtues and vices, for the feelings, and for attitudes. 'Courage', 'avarice', 'fear', 'jealousy', 'envy', 'pride', 'humility', and 'love' are all obvious examples. It may seem obvious why such terms should be used to refer not only to our emotions and feelings but also to character traits – to the dispositions to display these emotions and feelings. The reasons why we appraise these dispositions as virtues and vices may seem to be clear enough. But what is the connection of the names of emotions with the names of attitudes?

One answer has been offered by Roger Scruton. His suggestion is that both attitudes and emotions 'are expressed in directed behaviour; that is, behaviour of a consistent kind directed towards some object or class of objects'. Attitudes differ from emotions, however, in being '*founded* on belief, and a man can give up any attitude to the extent that he can give up the beliefs on which it is founded'. (1971, pp. 26–7) Emotions, on the other hand, are states in which 'desires and wishes tend to exist in the context of relatively few beliefs and of perhaps no definite intentions'. (p. 30) To this distinction Scruton adds another. It is an elaboration of Aristotle's distinction in the *Rhetoric* between emotions that have universal objects and those that have particular objects. Scruton writes:

94

Love and grief have particular objects. Others, such as contempt, admiration, and indignation, have universal objects. If I feel contempt for James, for example, it is because of something that is true about James; if that thing were true about William then I should feel contempt for William too. The object of my contempt is the particular – James – as an instance of the universal. . . . I would feel just the same toward anyone else who showed the same defect. (1980, pp. 525–6)

These claims are not quite correct, of course, since other qualities of William's – his youth or ignorance or ingenuousness, for example – might override or eliminate my contempt for him. I should 'feel just the same toward anyone else' only if all relevant circumstances were the same; and these could not be specified in advance.

Nevertheless, there is some such distinction between love and contempt. If I feel love for James I need not feel love for William simply because they share any given quality that I am able to recognize. Scruton remarks that, 'some mental states, therefore, are directed towards things as particulars, and some are directed towards things as tokens or instantiations of some type or property. We can know that X loves Y without identifying any quality of Y on the basis of which X loves him. . . . On the other hand, we cannot say that X despises Y unless it is possible to refer to some quality of Y towards which X's emotion is directed'. The ability to do this is the ability to provide a 'description in universal terms which might be satisfied by any one of an indefinite number of objects'. (1971, pp. 41–2) What conclusion does Scruton draw from these two distinctions? He believes that we should conclude that 'a mental state is most plausibly called an attitude if it contains some universal element'. 'For mental states directed towards particulars', he says, 'do not in general exhibit the coherence and rationality required for attitudes'. (p. 42) The reason why we refer to universal states as attitudes rather than emotions, therefore, is that if anything is the object of a universal state, then necessarily there is a reason for its being an object. Thus the demands for consistency and rationality that we make of attitudes, as against emotions, have some possibility of being satisfied. Scruton adds that there are a few universal states, such as shame and guilt, which are called emotions because of their 'prominent reactive content'. But 'most of those states which are normally called emotions – love, hatred, anger, depression – are particular in respect of their objects'. (p. 42)

Underlying these views there seems to be the notion that attitudes are essentially beliefs held with emotion – passionate beliefs – whereas the emotions are feelings – sensations and desires – given organization by beliefs. Both attitudes and emotions are exhibited in characteristic sorts of actions. True, Scruton does not state that attitudes must have an emotional component, but unless he believed that they usually do, there would be no need for him to spend time in drawing a distinction between emotions and attitudes. For if he believed that the latter were merely beliefs, then he ought to have concluded that there was no overlap between attitudes and emotions, and hence no danger of confusing one with the other. But in that case how could we account for the overlap between the names of the emotions and the names of attitudes?

It is certainly true that both emotions and attitudes are patterns of 'behaviour of a consistent kind directed towards some object'. However, it is untrue that attitudes are generally 'founded on belief' whereas emotions are not. Love, hatred, anger, depression – to take Scruton's examples – commonly incorporate beliefs that if altered also change the emotions founded on them. Love believed to be unrequited often turns into anger or depression, and anger that is discovered to be misdirected often turns into remorse. Even depression of unknown origin incorporates beliefs such as 'my life has nothing more of value to offer me'. It is as true of most emotions as it is of attitudes that a person can give them up to the extent that the underlying beliefs of both can be relinquished. If a belief in an imminent danger is given up, so is the fearful response. If the object of hate is believed to have been eliminated permanently, then the active hate directed at that object disappears. If the object of our indignation is believed to have made adequate restitution, our indignation abates. But love remains since its belief requirements are minimal.

On the other hand, while there is a genuine distinction to be found between states with particular objects and states with universal objects, this distinction does not run parallel to that between feeling-states (emotions) and belief-states (attitudes). Thus the sentence, 'My attitude toward my former husband is one of anger', can refer to a particular object: according to Scruton, the speaker need not 'feel just the same toward anyone else who showed the same defect'. Similarly the sentences, 'Her attitude toward her mother was one of affection and love', and 'His attitude toward his wife was that of pure hate', refer to particular objects for which there are no substitutes. That husband, that mother, and that wife are not, on Scruton's view, 'tokens or instantiations of some type or property'. Nevertheless, these particulars are the objects both of attitudes and emotions. Conversely, we can feel the emotions of love, hate, anger, or depression toward such universal objects as war, vivisection, fox-hunting, and religion. 'I hate war' was one of President F. D. Roosevelt's better known remarks. Was he expressing an attitude or an emotion, or both? Why not sometimes one and sometimes the other? Is fear of Europeans an attitude? Is my fear of Europeans an emotion when I tremble in their presence and an attitude when I simply contemplate their baleful influence on my tribe? These questions cannot be answered in terms of attitudes with universal objects and emotions with particular objects. •

EMOTIONAL AND NONEMOTIONAL ATTITUDES

The original and basic sense of 'attitude' is bodily posture or position, and a sentence such as 'Glen adopted a tolerant attitude toward his son's excesses' can mean that Glen displayed tolerance on a particular occasion. But, of course, we can also speak of a person's habitual or general or usual attitude, and in this qualified usage the person's attitude is a disposition or habitual tendency – a tendency toward a specific and established form of response, whether of action or thought. Hence to adopt a particular attitude, such as sexual tolerance, is to adopt, in the *O.E.D.*'s words, 'settled behaviour or manner of acting, as representative of feeling or opinion'. In saying, 'My attitude toward homosexuals is one of tolerance', I am understood to be referring to my general attitude and not merely to a display of tolerance on a particular occasion. I am announcing something like a general policy of thought and action, a policy that can be displayed in actual incidents. But on any given occasion it may not be clear to other people whether my tolerance is based on such a policy or is simply a general trait of my character or is limited to the occasion in general. Thus the sentence, 'Glen's attitude toward his son that morning was paternal', does not by itself enable us to decide whether the attitude is limited or general, policy-based or a trait of character.

The phrase 'attitude of' can be placed in front of any emotion name: There are attitudes of joy, grief, fear, anger, pride, and jealousy, for example. The reason why we can do this is that emotions are one kind of evaluative attitude, for the emotions, like attitudes in general, are forms of 'settled behaviour or manner of acting, as representative of feeling or opinion' – or of evaluative judgment. All emotions then, whether dispositional or occurrent, are attitudes toward their objects. But many attitudes have nothing to do with emotions since the latter are only one variety of the former. There are attitudes of indifference, neutrality, detachment, carelessness, scepticism, understanding, secretiveness, frankness, tolerance, conciliation, decency, honesty, and a great host of other character traits that are not themselves emotions and that need not incorporate any emotion. These examples show us that many attitudes are not beliefs held with emotion. Moreover, some nonemotional attitudes exhibit no more 'coherence and rationality' than do some emotions. Indifference, carelessness, secretiveness, and frankness, for instance, may be mere character traits and thus not based on policy. In such cases they may be as little under the control of coherent and explicit beliefs as the emotions of fear or anger, and sometimes less so. People usually know what they fear or are angry with, and ordinarily they know why; but careless or secretive people may not even know that they possess these traits, and hence not know why they have them. The beliefs that are exhibited in them need be neither rational nor consistent since the beliefs will not be under the agent's scrutiny.

Some beliefs about the appropriate situations in which any given attitude can or should be expressed are beliefs learned, initially at least, from the social group in which the agent is reared. In this respect many nonemotional attitudes resemble the emotional ones. The appropriate occasions for the display of such attitudes as frankness, tolerance, and conciliation are taught and learned – or not taught and not learned – in exactly the same ways as are the emotional attitudes of love, pride, and shame. Both sorts of attitudes are learned by children through learning – whether by example, participation, or instruction – when and when not to display instances of them. The learning process may not produce uniform results, for national festivals in which noble love of country is highly commended may instil only scepticism in some participants and sentimentality in others. But there is no difference on this point between emotional and nonemotional attitudes. To learn what attitude to take toward sneers, once they have been recognized, is no different in principle from learning what attitude to take toward the elderly, once they have been identified. In both cases the social group may fail to create in its young the desired attitude; in both cases the group may be divided in its preferences and have no one attitude to offer. Learning not to love one's neighbours may be as difficult, in some instances, as learning to love them.

Emotions, we have said, are one kind of evaluative attitude, the kind to which bodily sensations, physiological responses, and various states of feeling tone are attached as a matter of definition. Jerome Schaffer has put this familiar view of emotion briefly:

To undergo a particular emotion is, in this analysis, to undergo a particular kind of physiological and/or sensational state which was caused by a particular complex of belief and desire. What emotion it is will be determined by the kind of beliefs and desires and the kinds of physiological and sensational effects. (1983, p. 161)

Schaffer compares such a causal definition with that of 'scar', for a scar is 'a particular state of bodily tissue which was caused by an appropriate sort of prior injury'. (p. 162) The sensations and physiological effects in question are those such as blushing, facial pallor, stomach contractions, rapid heart-beat, panting, restlessness, muscular weakness, sweating, cravings, and chills. There are also general feeling tones such as those of buoyancy or depression – and, we should add, such nonbodily feelings as exultation, interest, and concern. The presence of at least some of these physical changes is necessary for the existence of an emotion as distinct from the existence of a mere attitude. The latter, like the former, consists in a set of beliefs, evaluations, and often desires, that are expressed in patterned behaviour that is directed toward an object. But plain attitudes lack the sensations and physiological effects that are, in part, caused by beliefs, evaluations, and desires in the case of the emotions. It is clear that the effectiveness of this characterization depends on distinguishing, as Schaffer does distinguish, desires as dispositions from the sensations and physiological effects that occur in such states as 'yearning, pining, longing, hankering, or craving'. (p. 168) Many desires produce neither such effects nor nonbodily feelings, and the frustration of desires need not produce them either.

100

The basic difference, then, between mere attitudes and emotions – between plain attitudes and coloured attitudes – is that of the absence or presence, respectively, of specifiable physical and psychological changes. The emotions proper are states in which such changes occur. Emotion-terms refer either to these states or to our dispositions to undergo them. Thus such terms as 'love', 'fear', 'jealousy', and 'pride' are sometimes used to refer to emotions and sometimes to plain attitudes, whereas other terms such as 'rage', 'fury', 'hate', and 'joy' are employed only for emotions. In their emotion-referring use these terms refer to characteristic physical changes partly caused by certain beliefs, appraisals, and desires, whereas in their purely attitudinal use they refer to those same appraisals, beliefs, and desires in the absence of physical changes. Since we often employ the same terms for both uses, and are thus sometimes reporting agitations and sometimes not, it can be unclear in particular cases whether any relevant physical change has been undergone. Quite commonly, it is not important to know this. If we say that a woman has been deeply affected by what has happened, we may mean that she has undergone physical sensations and had physiological effects of certain kinds in consequence of certain beliefs, appraisals, and desires; or we may mean only that she has been subject to those beliefs, appraisals, and desires, that they have altered or affected those that she held previously, and we leave open, as irrelevant, the question whether she has also been physically – that is emotionally – affected.

However, that certain terms have both a purely attitudinal use and a use for reporting the physical occurrences of emotions does not mean that we are constantly in doubt as to which use is being employed. It is true that the remark, 'I am happy that your tour has been successful' relies on its context for making it clear whether the speaker is actually happy or is merely being polite. But in the parenthetical uses to which Schaffer calls attention, as in 'You will, I fear, need deeper soil for your strawberries', or 'I regret to announce that bean noodles have been taken off today's menu', there is usually no reference to the speaker's emotional state, only to his or her beliefs and to the desire to be helpfully informative. (pp. 167–8) Anyone familiar with the conventions of such situations understands that these usages flow from the speaker's social role and not from personal agitation. Analogously, we can use the word 'love' either as a genuine term of endearment or as a term of conventional benevolence, as when the bus conductor says to a woman passenger, unknown to him, 'That will be eighty pence, love'. The initial *frisson* of such usages lasts only as long as the ambiguity remains unresolved. Sometimes, of course, it is not resolved, and then we cannot answer the question, 'Emotion-referring or not?' Did Roosevelt really, emotionally, hate war? Does my fear of Europeans consist in my being frightened of them or do I simply believe that their influence on my tribe will be for the worse? To answer such questions we need information that we may well not possess and have no practical means of obtaining. Nevertheless, if we had that information we could give satisfactory answers.

LOVING PARTICULAR VERSUS UNIVERSAL OBJECTS

Armed with Scruton's Aristotelian distinction between emotions that have universal objects and emotions that have particular objects, let us return to the question discussed much earlier in Chapter 1, under the heading What Does the Lover Love? There it was claimed that a difference exists between loving a person and loving that person's manifestation of certain qualities or properties; and it was also claimed that none of the answers to the original question accounted for this distinction. It was then suggested that since a lover often helps to create in his beloved the features that the lover hopes to find, and that the lover values, the agent's love can both precede and produce the belief that the partner is loved because of those features. In brief, it was implied that we quite commonly first love a person and then find in him or her some instantiated qualities that we can offer as explanation and justification of our love. On this account, it appears as though the lover is often drawn to the beloved by unconscious needs, desires, and wishes. Only later, after deeper acquaintance, does the lover identify, and perhaps create, in the beloved the qualities that satisfy those needs and desires. The difference, then, between loving a person and loving that person's exemplification of certain qualities looks to be, in part, a difference in the lover's knowledge over time. On this view, for someone to become lovingly attached to a person is, in part, for the agent to find in that person satisfying responses to some of the agent's unconscious needs and wishes. By contrast, for the agent to become lovingly attached to some of a person's characteristics is at least for the agent to identify and be drawn to them as satisfying some of the agent's needs and wishes, although the agent need not be able to specify those needs and wishes, either because they are unconscious or because the agent has not paid attention to them.

The obvious shortcoming of this account is that it makes the difference between loving a person and loving some of that person's qualities merely a matter of the increased knowledge possessed by the agent in the latter case. Yet this cannot be correct. For while the agent's ability to specify the qualities that are cherished in the beloved does represent an increase of knowledge, that increase is not the relevant difference. The increase in knowledge cannot explain why loving a person is not the same as loving some of that person's qualities. The fact that we must be able to identify the qualities in order to be able reasonably to assert that we love those particular qualities is a logical truism. But from this truism, and the additional fact that we can often give neither those qualities nor any other features as the reasons why we love a specific person, it does not follow that loving a person, as against loving some of that person's qualities, simply consists in a state of our not yet being able to identify those qualities, of our simply being ignorant of them. For even if we are drawn to our beloved by conscious needs, desires, and wishes, and can name at that time the qualities in the beloved that we believe will satisfy those desires, we are still simply itemizing the qualities that we love. Giving such a list, however, even when we can, is not the same – for reasons given previously – as saying why we love the entire person.

The distinction at issue here is that between loving a particular object and loving a universal object. If Scruton is correct, then the object of love is always particular. He gives no argument for this conclusion except to say that 'we can know that X loves Y without identifying any quality of Y on the basis of which X loves him'. If this is a claim that knowledge of Y's qualities is never needed, then Scruton might wish to go on to argue that we cannot love universal objects because this would amount, in any given case, to loving an indefinitely large number of items, namely, all those that satisfied the description of the universal. To love a quality or property, then, would be to love any instance of it only as an exemplification of a type and not for itself alone – not as a particular instance as distinct from other instances. Yet in the case of people, at least, we often claim to love only a particular instance. Given this fact, Scruton might challenge us to show how a person can possibly feel love or hate or anger toward a universal object such as a quality or a property or an activity. Can we really hate – or love – war as such?

The correct answer, we have said, is 'yes'. We can value qualities, activities, and other universal objects as inherently worthwhile or satisfying and thus to be cherished. For even though they do not have interests with which we can identify ourselves, as we can in the case of people, they can still possess a distinctive character that we can hold dear. We can desire their good for their sake, and not merely our own, in the

104

sense of desiring to ensure their existence and enlarge the number of their instances. Someone who genuinely loves war may value it as an activity that displays the noblest virtues of human beings: their courage, contempt for danger, joy in domination. War is taken to be the fullest and best expression of these qualities, and hence to be cherished and encouraged for its own sake. To claim that we cannot love war because that commits us to loving any instance of it – any specific war – only as an exemplification of a type, and not for itself alone, is a mistake. If the claim were correct, then we could never cherish a principle but only its instances; never a virtue, only its displays. But we can cherish and hold dear principles and virtues that are seldom, or perhaps never, adequately exemplified. It is because we do cherish them that we try to exemplify them, however hopeless the prospect: for example, when a person in the midst of a war tries to carry out the moral injunction, 'Treat all human life as sacred'.

Thus we can love both particular and universal objects. In loving the former we can value them both as unique individuals and as instances of cherished qualities. It is logically true that what we love only as an instance of a property or type we cannot also love as a particular or unique individual. But from this logical truism we cannot conclude that we can love only particular objects, that we cannot also love some of the properties that they exemplify. We can certainly love both the particular object, or individual, and some of the universals that the unique individual exemplifies. That is, we can love both the individual and some of its properties without loving the particular object merely because it possesses those properties. For we often cherish a person's exemplification of specific qualities while not cherishing the person as a whole; and, similarly, we often cherish the person as inherently worthwhile but actively dislike some, or even many, of the qualities that the person exemplifies. In such cases of dislike or love of certain qualities, we are certainly committed to disliking or loving the indefinitely large number of their instances simply because they are instances. However, this fact does not prevent any given instance from also having a unique temporal and spatial relationship with instances of other qualities or properties. It is that unique relationship – or set of unique relationships –that constitutes, in part, the particular object of one person's love for another. The same holds of some of the other emotions such as hate and grief.

Hence it is true that when the agent loves another person, and not merely some of that person's qualities, the agent is cherishing, in part, a particular complex of instantiated qualities. It is a complex, however, that is made unique for the agent and the partner by occurring at certain times and places, and by thus having an unrepeatable career or history. It is a complex composed, in part, of what the agent takes to be some of the partner's tendencies and capacities, whether the latter are fully realized or still potential. These tendencies and capacities, since they can be physical, psychological, or moral, require time for their display and development. So it is often the case that the lover cherishes their past, present, and future states. The lover can also cherish those of his or her own complementary or matching capacities that are called forth by the traits of the beloved; and in consequence the lover can regard this influence as a highly valued and irreplaceable element in the relationship. In committing himself or herself to the furtherance of these processes, the lover relies upon the couple's joint ability to create an outcome that each partner finds satisfying and valuable enough to maintain or to develop further.

To claim that in loving another person the lover is cherishing, in part, a particular complex of instantiated qualities is not to reduce the object of the love to an especially full, and hence unrepeatable, instantiated complex of qualities. The reason why love for a particular person is not reducible to an unrepeatable instantiated complex of qualities is this: To love a particular person is often to commit oneself to an

106

open-ended relationship. It is, we have said, not merely to love the present person or to love that person as one who has a specific history. It is also to be prepared to love the person in the future despite – or because of – the many changes that may take place in the character and circumstances of the beloved. Since the details of such a commitment cannot be specified in advance, the complete and final character of the relationship between the lover and the object of love cannot, at any given time, be specified. That can be done only when the relationship is finished. Similarly, the object of love cannot, at a particular time, be identical with a specifiable complex of qualities. The complex is essentially incomplete, and hence so is the object of love. Thus both the latter and the relationship itself are incompletely specifiable. Of course, once they belong completely to the past we can, in principle, identify all the qualities embodied in the relationship and all those qualities for which the beloved was cherished. But all such qualities were uniquely instantiated, spatially and temporally; and what is being suggested here is that in loving someone or something we can, and sometimes do, cherish both the incompletely specifiable beloved and the unique relationship that holds between the beloved and the lover. When the relationship is finished, we can say what it amounted to – if we have the necessary information – but while the relationship is in progress, and we are committed to its continuance, we cannot know what qualities we shall discover in the beloved and in ourselves; or what the features of the relationship will turn out to be. The same is true of some other social relations, of course, such as that of friend, or consort, or patron. In all such cases, no reduction of them to a complex of specifiable qualities is possible.

However, it is also true that a living person can maintain love for a dead person and that the relationship can then no longer be open-ended. But it is not being claimed that all cases of love for a person are open-ended, for we can continue actively to love not only the dead and absent but the person

107

who Mini once was and no longer closely resembles. Moreover, we can invent aspects of, and indeed an entire relationship with, someone whom we have never known or who does not exist. These inventions can be open-ended in the sense that their creator cannot predict the outcome. But open-ended commitment to the fantasy-figure of one's own creation in the future is very different from the lover's commitment to what the beloved may become – to the possible changes in another, and thus independent, agent whose actions will require appropriate responses from the lover.

Now the agent may be able to tell us, or somehow make clear to us by a variety of other means, some of the many ways in which the beloved instantiates the qualities of one sort of person. In doing this, however, Max will not be giving us a description of Mini that provides him with reasons for loving her. For we have suggested that what helps to constitute his love, and is also part of what he loves, is their unique relationship with each other: their joint history, their understanding of – and sympathy toward – each other's unrealized capacities, their reliance upon each other's commitment, their view of their common future. To offer an account of these alone as the individuating description under which Max loves Mini would simply be to repeat the details of their life together, and thus the full course of their relationship. But even though all these details taken together form a history of their relationship, at best they individuate the relationship, not the beloved Mini alone. Her life is entwined with his; any attempt to individuate her as one of the partners in that life will result in characterizing their relationship in contrast to other relationships. Therefore in claiming to love the whole person, Mini, the lover, Max, is actually claiming also to love what he takes to be their unique relationship with each other rather than merely some of the qualities that Mini happens to exemplify. So in contrasting love of some of a person's qualities with love of that person as an individual, we are contrasting love of specifiable qualities with love of a person

108

who occupies a unique relationship that has been, and may continue to be, formed over time by the two agents.

Of course not all cases of a close relationship are of this sort; there are innumerable sorts of intimate relationships in which love of the partner's qualities plays the dominating role. In these cases admiration, respect, and envy can often be singled out as necessary elements. Sometimes in such cases the partners characterize their relationship as one in which each loves what the other 'stands for', that is the qualities or principles or roles that each partner exemplifies for the other. Thus there is a familiar distinction between loving what the partner stands for and loving the partner. While the same person can often do both, this is not always so. Sometimes the partners in a relationship are bonded together in such a way as to desire only each other's good, and yet each can dislike almost all the qualities and moral principles that the other is taken to exemplify. On occasion, wives of alcoholic husbands are themselves neurotically bound in the marriage, but even their joint recognition of this fact need not prevent the two partners from wishing to remain together for what each believes to be the benefit of the other.

Here it might be interjected that the presence of a unique and irreplaceable relationship between people obviously does not ensure that they will evaluate it as being worthwhile in itself to them. Yet only if they do so can they love one another and unite their interests. However, not all relationships thought to be unique and irreplaceable by the participants are also valued by them; and of those unique relationships that are valued by their participants, some have nothing to do with love. Two people can hate each other in such a way that if one were to die the other would lose interest in life. Each partner may value the relationship as worthwhile in itself because it provides a goal to which the partner can be fully committed – the destruction of the other. There are also relations of benevolent friendship that are taken to be both irreplaceable and valuable but whose participants limit their

109

commitment well short of full-fledged love. On the other hand, there are many irreplaceable relationships to which some of the participants attach little or no value: Some people, for example, are pleased at the death of their burdensome parents; some parents neglect their children; and some people who are cherished as irreplaceable by their lovers do not return the sentiment.

THE LOVABLE AND THE FEARSOME

Of the questions asked in the Introduction, one remains to be answered. It is whether love occupies a special position among the emotions because there appear to be so few restrictions on what can be loved. Yet there are, we said, equally few constraints on what we can fear. However, in the case of the latter, it was said, we can usually give explanatory reasons why we fear something or someone but quite commonly are unable to give explanatory reasons for our loves. Similarly, it might be said, we can usually give justificatory reasons for our fearing something but, much less often, for our loving something. Indeed, it has sometimes been suggested that the very notion of justifying our loves is mistaken because there is no class of inherently lovable items as there is of inherently fearsome ones. In consequence, no one is called upon to justify love of something, for there is no way of showing it to be unlovable in principle or by nature. In contrast, there are things that because they threaten the peace and safety of human beings are by their very nature fearsome. Starvation, drowning, physical assault, and natural calamities such as cyclones and earthquakes, are universally feared. But infants, domestic animals, marriage partners, ample food, and calm weather are not universally loved: Sometimes they are disliked and sometimes they are merely tolerated. This difference between love and fear, according to the view in question, explains why we can be more easily criticized for what we fear then for what we love. This same difference

110

also explains why we can supply explanatory reasons for the former but not for the latter. In the case of fear we can rely on a common, and hence objective, evaluation of which objects are appropriately feared. To fear something that is commonly agreed to be harmless is to be irrational.

The situation is quite different in the case of love. William Lyons puts the matter thus:

> With an emotion such as love, and presumably its opposite, hate, and possibly the emotion embarrassment, there does not seem to be any objective norm as to what is to count as an acceptable or rational evaluation, or by which one could predict what sort of properties are being picked out and evaluated. To take love, there is no principle or set of principles which tells a person whom he is likely to find appealing or 'good in his eyes' in the way that there are principles or generalisations as to what things are likely to be dangerous to humans. Who a person is drawn to seems to be very much a matter for the individual person. . . . There is no common-sense view about who is appealing in the matter of love. . . . It is very difficult to make good a case that the object of someone's love could not really be appealing to him or her.
>
> So while we can predict, up to a point, what sort of things a person will be afraid of – such things as being inside the lion's cage at the zoo, swimming in areas where there is a strong undertow – we cannot predict what sort of person somebody will fall in love with, unless of course we explicitly or implicitly know this particular person's past history in this matter. (1980, pp. 78–9)

In part, this account is clearly mistaken. It is not true that there are some things that everyone fears. What is true is that some things are generally agreed to be dangerous under certain conditions: Strong undertow and the inside of a cage filled with lions are two of them. However, not all apparently dangerous things are feared by all people. Many people, either by training, self-discipline, ignorance, or recklessness, confront the most dangerous situations with equanimity, including those that threaten the destruction of the agent and of all that the agent holds dear. Unless we know an agent's past history in this matter we cannot accurately predict the kinds of things that will make the agent afraid, even when

111

there is general agreement as to the degree of risk. Among lion trainers a cage of lions may be thought dangerous but not frightening; among strong and experienced surfers a strong undertow need not even be dangerous, much less feared. What a person finds frightening, as against objectively dangerous or risky under certain conditions, depends very much on that person's history. There is no set of principles that by itself will tell us that both the Eskimos and the Tahitians will find snowstorms frightening. After all, the agent's degree of fear in a situation depends on a personal assessment of its degree of risk, and that assessment is determined by the agent's view as to his or her ability to cope with the situation. Ignorance of the danger or risk commonly produces lack of fear; but knowledge of risk, when accompanied by the agent's belief in the agent's own competence, need not produce fear.

Just as there is a class of items that most people find inherently dangerous or risky, so there is a class of items that most people find inherently worthwhile: These include character qualities such as loyalty, trustworthiness, and sympathy; personal relationships such as those of friendship or love; activities that call forth people's most developed skills and abilities; and objects that either display those abilities or strikingly reveal the organization of nature. Nevertheless, ignorance, apathy, lack of education, poor judgment, or passion, often lead people not to recognize – or even if they do so, not to cherish – particular instances of the sorts of things that in general they acknowledge to be intrinsically worthwhile to them. Here again, there is no set of principles that by itself will allow us to predict which person will cherish a particular item, or what ranking the person will give to a particular sort of item drawn from the class of things commonly thought to be worthwhile in themselves. Accurate prediction of the individual case requires us to have information about the history of the agent in question. Any given item's degree of appeal for the agent can be fixed partly by the agent's as-

112

sessment of the extent to which it instantiates a valued type of item, partly by the item's special relationship to the agent, and partly by the rank held by that type, or individual item, in the agent's preference schedule. It is extremely common for two people to agree on one or more of these points but not on all.

Thus there is often widespread agreement, especially within a particular society, on what sorts of things are intrinsically worthwhile and yet general disagreement as to their ranking. Moreover, this agreement is often combined with an additional widespread disagreement as to whether a particular example is a good illustration of its sort. This latter fact encourages the view put forward by Lyons that 'who a person is drawn to seems to be very much a matter for the individual person. . . . There is no commonsense view about who is appealing in the matter of love'. Nevertheless, there is usually general agreement, at least within a society, on the sorts of people who are appealing: those who are physically attractive, generous, loyal, sympathetic, gentle, honest, for example. But exactly who embodies these qualities, and to what extent, is often a matter of general disagreement.

REASONS FOR LOVING AND FEARING

In Chapter 1, under Love-Comprising Relationships and Public Criteria, it was remarked that love-comprising relations such as caring, respecting, and attraction are not alone in lacking objective public criteria. Many other psychological and moral concepts also lack such criteria: Among them are loyalty, sympathy, trustworthiness, greed, generosity, esteem, and courage. Despite this lack of standard tests for the presence of such qualities, the members of a given society are usually, or at least often, able to reach some agreement on the presence of these qualities in the general run of cases. This is possible because the members have learned the use of these concepts by being taught them under common conditions. What they have not – and could not have – been taught under these common conditions is how to apply concepts of this type so as to reach consensus on the extent to which they are exemplified in every given case. All of them can be instantiated in an endless variety of ways that depend upon social conventions, the special circumstances of the occasion, and the character of the agent. If we standardized the criteria for these concepts, we should not only reduce to fixed forms the ways in which the concepts could be expressed, but we should stop their further development. We should then not be able to recognize the new forms in which greed or courage or loyalty might be expressed. So it must remain a matter of individual judgment and discrimination – that is, argument – as to whether a particular action is one of outstanding courage or of considerable recklessness; whether someone has displayed only sympathy or sympathy mixed with self-interest.

The case of love is similar although more complex. Relations such as caring, respecting, and attracting certainly have no public criteria for the degree to which they are exemplified in any given instance, and since love between people commonly includes these relations, any example of love itself will lack such criteria. In addition, there are and can be no standard tests for the presence or extent of the other elements that comprise the lovers' unique relationship: their sympathy toward, and understanding of, each other's unrealized capacities, their reliance upon each other's commitment, their shared affection for common activities in the past, and their shared hopes for the future. Even if we were to try to provide criteria for each of these elements, we should still have the problem of combining them into a usable set of criteria for the presence and extent of the relationship of love itself.

Thus the distinction, in the case of love, between agreement on the types of things that are taken to be worthwhile in themselves and disagreement on their exemplars runs parallel to that discussed in the case of fear: namely, general agreement on objective danger and common disagreement on particular examples of the fearful. We can only fear what we take to be dangerous to us in some respect, and we can only love what we take to be inherently worthwhile in some respect. To love what we took to be completely worthless would be like fearing what we thought was completely harmless. We can certainly love what we think is worthless or dangerous or evil in many respects. But if we think it wholly evil or worthless, then what we love is not the object itself but something associated with it, such as the physical and mental state into which we are put or some feature of the situation in which the object is embedded. Unconsciously based fears and loves are not a counter-example to this. For when their actual objects are brought to light they turn out to be of this linked sort. The two cases of fear and love are thus similar in that we may not be able to state precisely what it is that we fear or love in a situation; and we often do not know precisely why we fear something or why we love something. It is not true, then, that we find it easier to give explanatory and justificatory reasons for our fears than we do for our loves. The belief to the contrary is often based on the view that has just been rejected: There are objective norms for evaluating what is frightening, but there are no such norms for evaluating what is appealing. Once we reject this view, it becomes clear that insofar as we can know the object of our fear, we can also know the object of our love. To the extent that there are dispositional or occurrent fears whose object is simply a possible but unknown danger, so there are dispositional or occurrent loves whose object is simply a possible but unknown item of inherent worthiness.

Similarly, it is no more – and sometimes no less – difficult for a person to give an explanatory reason for his or her dispositional loves than it is for dispositional fears. Someone who is afraid of snakes, women, and thunder may or may not be able to tell us how he came to develop these phobias and why they persist. Yet exactly the same is true of someone who loves snakes, women, and thunder: He may or may not know the psychological origin of these dispositions and why he continues to have them. In the case both of fears and loves the actual explanation may be different from that given by the agent.

So the claim that we can usually give explanatory reasons why we fear – or love – something is ambiguous. Sometimes it refers to occurrent fears or loves and sometimes to dispositional ones. Often we can give explanations for neither sort. On those occasions when we can and do give explanatory reasons, our reasons vary according to the type of question being asked. The question 'Why are you afraid?' may mean

1. 'What is the situation that is now creating a state of fear in you?'
2. 'Why does that situation put you in that state?'
3. 'What is the sort of situation that you are disposed to fear?'
4. 'Why do you have a disposition to fear that sort of situation?'

In parallel fashion, the question 'Why do you feel love?' may mean

5. 'What object has put you into a state of love?'
6. 'Why does that object do that to you?'
7. 'What is the sort of object that you are disposed to love?'
8. 'Why are you disposed to love that sort of object?'

As long as we interpret the two questions 'Why are you afraid?' and 'Why do you feel love?' in parallel fashion, their answers will run parallel to each other. It is only when we compare the answer to question (1), for example, with the answer to question (6) that the two answers diverge in type. We then conclude that since the answer to question (1) tells us what object the agent is afraid of, whereas question (6) is often difficult to answer, we can explain why we fear something but not why we love something. In fact, we have asked different types of questions in the two cases. If we had asked

(1) and (5) together or (2) and (6) together, our answers would have raised parallel problems and given parallel explanations.

The case is similar with respect to justificatory reasons except that there are only two interpretations of each of the questions 'Why are you afraid?' and 'Why do you feel love?' One interpretation is 'What good reason is there for that situation now to create in you a state of fear (love)?' The other is 'What good reason is there for you to have a disposition to fear (love) that sort of situation?' The first asks what justification you have for a particular situation to produce a state of occurrent fear (or love) in you. The second asks what justification you have for being disposed to fear (or love) a particular sort of situation. Both justifications may be difficult to supply, but there is no difference of difficulty as between love and fear. Whatever good reasons we have for being disposed to fear women or crowds or Russians will not differ in type from the good reasons we have, if any, for being disposed to love women, crowds, and Russians. Nor will there be any typological difference in our justification for being terrified by a neighbour's dog last Sunday and our justification for suddenly being overcome with affection for that neighbour's wife the next day. Hence if love occupies a special position among the emotions, it is not because we have some special difficulty in explaining and justifying our loves. In that respect they do not differ from our fears. In both fear and love there are few constraints on their objects – although fewer for love than for fear – and equal constraints on their explanatory and justificatory reasons.

CRITICIZING THE LOVER'S JUDGMENTS OF INHERENT WORTH

Now against this conclusion it is often argued that there is an obvious reason why a person's love, in contrast to other emotions, cannot be called reasonable or unreasonable, however fortunate or suitable, inappropriate, odd, foolish, or

117

risky it might be. The reason is that someone's love for another person incorporates evaluations of inherent worth whereas other emotions do not. In George Pitcher's words, these evaluations 'are, in a manner of speaking indefensible: for in them, something is deemed good in itself. The man in love wants, for example, to be with his beloved; and he wants this simply because he enjoys her company for its own sake – there is no reason for it, he just wants to be with her'. (1965, p. 341) It is this evaluation, says Pitcher, that can be called neither reasonable nor unreasonable; for such an evaluation, 'there can be, within wide limits, neither standards of criticism nor justifying reasons'. (p. 342)

Here we must distinguish three different questions that arise from Pitcher's remarks. One question is whether, in general, evaluations of intrinsic worth can be subject to rational criticism. A second question is whether evaluations of intrinsic worth applied to individual cases of love are subject to standards of criticism. A third question is whether love, which incorporates such evaluations, differs from some – or all – of the other emotions in this respect. Clearly, it is the latter two questions that bear most directly upon our present topic, for we are considering the specific claim that love differs from most of the other emotions because it incorporates evaluations of inherent worth. Even if we produced an argument to the effect that no evaluations of inherent worth are subject to rational criticism, we should still have to show that while any given case of love includes them, cases of the other emotions do not. The general question of whether, and in what respects, all such evaluations are subject to rational criticism is much too extensive to be discussed here: It is a basic question of ethics and esthetics, and not one that can be dealt with here except in passing.

Pitcher says that there is no 'clear sense' to the claim that one person's love for another can be rational or irrational, reasonable or unreasonable. To answer the question 'Why do you want to be with her all the time?' with the reply 'Because

I love her' is to rule out some reasons but not to supply one. My preference for my beloved, like my 'preference for chocolate over vanilla ice cream', is an evaluation for which there can be no justificatory reasons. (pp. 341–2)

The soundness of this claim depends upon the sense given to the phrase 'reasonable or unreasonable' and whether it is to be applied to the agents' beliefs or behaviour. Suppose that Mini believes that she loves Max even though she thinks him to be wicked, bad, and basically evil. It is not that she believes some one aspect of him is morally good, or otherwise attractive but not evil, and hence worthy of her love. Rather, she believes that she is irresistibly attracted to, and thus highly values, what is evil in him. She realizes that it is extremely odd for her to find appealing and attractive what she takes to be morally bad. Of course she does not realize that her love is not of Max and that what actually appeals to her is the relief from guilt feelings that the relationship gives her: She uses his evil ways as a means of punishing, and hence purifying, herself. But of such a case are we to say that Mini's evaluation of Max is not unreasonable, that it is not irrational of her to believe herself to be strongly drawn to someone whom she finds morally detestable, and worse yet, to be drawn to him simply because, as she thinks, he is so thoroughly evil? If it is not unreasonable for an agent to believe that she loves what the agent herself acknowledges to be evil – to believe that she loves what she is otherwise committed to rejecting –then what is?

One example of unreasonableness given by Pitcher is that of a father being angry because his daughter wishes 'to go to a perfectly respectable dance', for it is not reasonable to think that her desire is wicked. Another example is that of a man who becomes extremely angry with his son over some trivial matter. The man's anger is disproportionate to the seriousness of his son's action. (p. 340) But if these two examples display the agents' unreasonable evaluations – the first mistaking a harmless wish for a harmful desire, and the second a trivial event for a major matter – then surely it is irrational for an agent to believe that she loves, and thus finds inherently worthwhile, someone whom she takes to be morally vicious. She believes that she is valuing as good in itself something that in the same respect she believes to be bad.

That a person, in this case a woman, can actually behave in this way – as against believing that she can – has often been denied, and correctly so. Aquinas, for example, wrote:

Evil is never loved except under some good description: i.e. a thing which is good from some secondary point of view is sometimes looked on as good pure and simple. . . . It is in this sense that a man 'loves evil-doing': by doing evil he can obtain some desirable thing, such as pleasure, money, or the like. (1963, p. 75)

Our present case is of this sort. For in it the agent appears to love an evil man because she actually thinks him good 'from some secondary point of view' – because by loving him she 'can obtain some desirable thing, such as pleasure, money, or the like.' The desirable thing she can obtain is relief from a punitive conscience. She appears to love evil, and does so because she has guilt feelings and wishes to be punished for her sins, real or imaginary. She tries to justify and explain these feelings of guilt by embracing what she takes to be evil. It is unquestionable that a person can hold these unreasonable beliefs and behave in this irrational way, for there is no practical impediment to someone making evaluations that are in conflict with one another. (Stocker, 1979, pp. 738–53) So there is a clear sense in which Mini's belief that she loves Max is unreasonable: Her estimate of her attitude toward him is mistaken and does not meet the requirements of sound judgment.

THE GROUNDS FOR CRITICIZING THE LOVER'S JUDGMENTS

There are a number of other objections that can be made to Pitcher's remarks. First, though not perhaps foremost, is that people are not always correct in the judgments that they make of things' inherent worth for them. For example, if a man says that he wishes to be with his beloved because he enjoys her company for its own sake, he may simply be mistaken. He may enjoy her company because she exerts a calming effect on his anxiety; if the effect disappears so will his enjoyment of her company. One way, then, of rationally criticizing the agent's judgment is to point out that his evaluation does not apply to what he takes it to apply to: that, for example, his judgment applies to the effects of his partner's company and not to her companionship itself. His evaluation is not of her inherent worth for him but of her utility as a means to something else that he takes to be inherently worthwhile. So the mere claim, by the agent or anyone else, that he finds something in particular to be good (or evil) in itself need not be accepted unchallenged.

Second, at least some initial judgments of inherent worth can be altered by the agent taking into account additional factors, including those characterized in opposing judgments and evaluations. Sometimes, of course, the agent's evaluation, to his or her own surprise, changes by itself over a period of time with no apparent external cause or reason. Mini discovers that she no longer prefers chocolate to vanilla ice cream and that she is no longer in love with Max. She no longer enjoys his company for its own sake although she cannot say why this is so: He is simply boring whereas he was once fascinating. Her therapist may be able to give a psychological explanation of the change by pointing out that her emotional needs, and hence preferences, have changed as a result of her reactions to her recent experiences. But while the therapeutic account may be causally correct, it need not provide any justificatory – morally justicatory – reasons for her change of attitude. Her partner is entitled to ask whether, given this unjustified alteration, she ever really loved him, whether she ever really valued him for his sake or whether she merely took her need to display affection as being a genuine love of him.

Often, however, the process of change takes place as a result, at least in part, of argument, scrutiny, and deliberation. Sometimes we can even be argued out of our current preference for chocolate as against vanilla ice cream. If we learn, for instance, that cocoa has been discovered to be dangerously carcinogenic, we may find that chocolate ice cream no longer has its formerly innocent flavour; our tongue searches the ice cream for poisonous elements and we have difficulty in forcing it down. The flavour that earlier struck us as rich and aromatic now seems to be indigestably sweet, and the fatty chocolate lies heavily on our stomach. New information has altered our evaluation and our judgment of inherent worth. Similarly, Mini's preference for Max can disappear when she learns that he is already a bigamist. Her evaluation of him was based on misinformation about his truthfulness. When her ignorance is corrected, her judgment of his worth may change accordingly. True, her evaluation of him need not alter, but it may be possible to find out what circumstances would make it do so; and if we can discover this, then her judgment of him may well be open to rational criticism. In short, her evaluation can be based on beliefs about him that may prove to be false. If the agent can be convinced of their falsity, then she will either have to embrace self-deception, find new supporting beliefs, or change her evaluation. Since all three outcomes can result from changes in her beliefs about Max, her evaluation of him as inherently worthwhile is at least subject to, if not actually changed by, rational challenge.

In similar fashion we can, and do, argue that it is irrational for someone to love – or even to claim to love – a person known only by description. We say that if Max has never met Mini and has never corresponded with her, and yet claims to have fallen in love with her after seeing her photograph, then he can only love a figure of his own fantasy. His attachment to Mini is a paradigm of irrationality. Again, if a man 'loves' his highly sociable wife in such a way that he imprisons her in a room so that no other man or woman can be tempted by her beauty, there is something flagrantly unreasonable about his jealous attachment. It is not merely that his jealous action is unreasonable, but that the sort of 'love' that produces such an action is itself open to criticism for that reason. Attachment of that kind, we say, is deplorable, for it does not properly value the beloved as an agent. It is attachment that destroys one of the conditions necessary for its own further development and is thus self-defeating. But self-defeating activities are models of unreasonableness.

Nevertheless, the fact that people's evaluations of things as inherently worthwhile are judgments open to rational criticism does not show that all evaluations of inherent worth always have, demand, or require justificatory reasons. They do not. This is because evaluations of inherent worth raise questions of their rationality, or of their reasonableness, only if the circumstances under which they are made appear to be unusual or unsatisfactory in some specifiable way: That is, they are made under circumstances in which their usual presuppositions are not met. As our examples have shown, conditions in which self-defeating activities, fantasy, false beliefs, new information, and character change are present lead us to question the evaluations that are associated with them. When there is no reason to believe that such disturbing conditions are present, there is also no reason for an agent to give any justificatory support for the judgments of what the agent finds inherently worthy. In the ordinary course of events, an agent does not have to justify — justify in the sense either of defending or supporting — judgments of inherent worthiness. The agent is at liberty to find all sorts of things and people inherently worthwhile or valuable or satisfying. If there is nothing specifiably unsatisfactory about the circumstances in which he or she does so, then there are no additional supporting circumstances left to describe. Unless there is something wrong with the conditions under which the evaluation is made, there is nothing to put right.

Of course it is true that the agent's act of valuing the loved

123

person can be given a causal explanation. But the valuation itself ordinarily cannot, and hence need not, be supported by reasons that somehow provide evidence or arguments in its favour. If there is nothing odd or peculiar about the attachment of Mini and Max, then to ask them to justify as rational their love of each other is simply to demand that they find some reason why they should – or perhaps be permitted to – love each other. But they do not love each other because they have decided to do so. As Zeno Vendler has noted, loving is not an action, and hence cannot be done deliberately and carefully; nor can we be held responsible for it as we can for an action (1967, p. 106), although we can, of course, be held responsible for acting from love in certain immoral ways. Hence Mini and Max ordinarily do not have, and cannot have, justificatory reasons – considerations that they take into account – for loving each other. With respect to love, they are patients, not actors, and as patients they do not have reasons for being acted upon – reasons, that is, for being, with respect to love, patients rather than actors. No such choice is available to them.

THE DISTINCTIVENESS OF LOVE

It is Pitcher's view that most emotions differ from love in that they do not incorporate the agent's evaluations of inherent worth. In hatred, for example, a person who hates a man wishes him ill-fortune, avoids meeting him, and should like to be rude to him. The agent does so because of believing such things as that the hated person has done something evil to the agent or possesses a morally worthless character. Pitcher writes:

Unlike love-evaluations, none of these hate-evaluations is a straightforward evaluation of something as good (or evil, for that matter) in itself. And there are generally accepted standards by which they can be judged: for example, when it is known what Q's actions have been, there would be general agreement, on the part of disinterested observers, as to whether or not Q had done something *evil* against P, and if so, as to how bad, how serious, it was. This means that a man's hatred, unlike his love, can be deemed reasonable or unreasonable. (1965, p. 342)

Yet it seems clear that some emotions – hate, grief, joy, and admiration, for instance – do incorporate at least some evaluations by the agent of inherent worth. Aristotle in the *Rhetoric* remarks that 'whereas anger arises from offences against oneself, enmity may arise even without that; we may hate people merely because of what we take to be their character. Anger is always concerned with individuals – a Callias or a Socrates – whereas hatred is directed also against classes: we all hate any thief and any informer'. (1984, 1382a 2–6, p. 2201) We can hate thievery and informing as evil in themselves since their practice is a rejection of social bonds. We can also hate as inherently evil such things as war, cruelty, intolerance, arrogance, injustice, or, as Marx did, servility. The same considerations arise for hatred as arise for love. An agent is as much at liberty to find types of actions, qualities, situations, and people to be inherently evil as to find other types – or at other times the same types – to be inherently good. A person's evaluation of cruelty, for instance, as evil in itself is like valuing love as entirely good. Thus on Pitcher's reasoning, hatred of a universal object as inherently evil ought to be deemed neither reasonable nor unreasonable since, according to him, there are no 'generally accepted standards' by which such evaluations can be judged.

Similarly, we can hate as inherently evil not only universal objects but also particular objects; and we can hate the latter for reasons that run parallel to those that support our love of a particular object. Thus if I feel hate for Mini, I need not feel hate for Ann simply because the two women share any given quality that I am able to recognize. I can simply come to hate as inherently evil, as I might otherwise come to love as inherently good, the person Mini who has a unique relationship with me. I can hate as inherently evil, as I might

125

have loved for its own sake, the unique entwinement of our two lives. Hatred, then, is on all fours with love: Both are open to the same forms of rational criticism, and both are subject to such criticism only if disturbing conditions are thought to be present.

Nor is hatred the only other emotion that can incorporate evaluations of inherent worthiness or unworthiness. We can admire – that is, take delight in and approve of – such universal objects as loyalty, courage, magnanimity, and self-respect – admire them not for their instrumental use but because we think them worthwhile in themselves. Of course, we can also admire, as we can also love, individual examples of these universal objects: an individual action, a piece of work, a person, a tradition, an organization. In admiring these examples we are also evaluating what we take to be the inherent worth of the qualities that the examples reveal. In the case of contempt, the opposite of admiration, our disdain of the qualities revealed in a given action – meanness, servility, and cowardice, for example – is the result of our evaluation of them as inherently worthless. Similarly, in the case of grief our sorrow is the outcome of our judgment that we have lost someone or something inherently worthwhile, just as in the case of joy we often celebrate the arrival or occurrence of something that we value for its own sake.

It is obvious, then, that emotions differ in the degree to which they incorporate judgments of inherent worth, and differ also in the extent to which their objects are particular or universal. But love is certainly not unusual among emotions in the degree to which it contains evaluations of inherent worth. Neither is it unusual in having both particular and universal objects. What makes love unusual among the emotions is the human inability to do without it – whether its bestowal or receipt – and the immense amount of satisfaction that love commonly brings to the people concerned. Of no other emotion do both of these features seem to hold. Some emotions such as grief, greed, hate, envy, jealousy, shame, remorse, fear, and anger, seem to give little permanent satisfaction and seem to be, under conditions not difficult to specify, largely dispensable. Other emotions such as joy, pride, and admiration give satisfaction to the agent but are dispensable in human life. Only love is both completely indispensable to the functioning of human society and a source of the fullest satisfaction known to human beings – despite the fact that loving or being loved often produces as much pain as it does pleasure. For love is always subject to frustration and rejection, and commonly bound together with such dangerous emotions as jealousy, hate, and fear. But this fact merely emphasizes that the beloved can be valued as having inherent worth even when giving pain and not simply when giving pleasure.

Works cited

Abraham, K. (1942) The Psycho-Sexual Differences between Hysteria and Dementia Praecox, in *Selected Papers on Psycho-Analysis*, London: Hogarth.

Aquinas, St. Thomas. (1963) *Summa Theologiae*, vol. 19, London: Eyre & Spottiswoode.

Aristotle. (1984) *Complete Works*, 2 vols., ed. J. Barnes, Princeton University Press.

Bedford, E. (1957) Emotions, *Proceedings of the Aristotelian Society*, 57.

Colette. (1955) *Chéri*, New York: Signet.

De Sousa, R. (1980) Self-Deceptive Emotions, in *Explaining Emotions*, ed. A. O. Rorty, Berkeley: University of California Press.

Eliot, G. (1965) *Middlemarch*, Harmondsworth: Penguin.

Fenichel, O. (1946) *The Psychoanalytic Theory of Neuroses*, London: Routledge.

Fisher, S. (1973) *The Female Orgasm*, London: Allen Lane.

Fontane, T. (1962) *Effi Briest*, London: New English Library.

Fortenbaugh, W. (1975) *Aristotle on Emotion*, London: Duckworth.

Freud, S. (1953) Group Psychology and the Analysis of the Ego, in *The Standard Edition of the Complete Psychological Works of Sigmund Freud*, trans. J. Strachey, et al., vol. 28, London: Hogarth.

Goldberg, S. L. (1983) Agents and Lives: Making Moral Sense of People, *The Critical Review*, 25, Canberra: Australian National University.

Goldman, A. (1976) Plain Sex, *Philosophy and Public Affairs*, 6.

Hamlyn, D. (1978) The Phenomena of Love and Hate, *Philosophy*, 53.

Hunter, J. F. M. (1983) *Thinking about Sex and Love*, New York: St. Martin's.

Kubie, L. (1960) *Practical and Theoretical Aspects of Psychoanalysis*, New York: Praeger.

Lyons, W. (1980) *Emotion*, Cambridge University Press.

Newton-Smith, W. (1973) A Conceptual Investigation of Love, in

Philosophy and Personal Relations, ed. A. Montefiore, London: Routledge.

Pitcher, G. (1965) Emotion, *Mind*, 74.

Powell, A. (1970) *Casanova's Chinese Restaurant*, London: Fontana.

Quinton, A. (1973) *The Nature of Things*, London: Routledge.

Russell, B. (1967) *The Autobiography of Bertrand Russell*, vol. 1, London: Allen and Unwin.

Schaffer, J. (1983) An Assessment of Emotion, *American Philosophical Quarterly*, 20.

Schnitzler, A. (n.d.) The Man of Honour, reprinted in *Vienna: Games with Love and Death*, Harmondsworth: Penguin.

Scruton, R. (1971) Attitudes, Beliefs and Reasons, in *Morality and Moral Reasoning*, ed. J. Casey, London: Methuen.

Scruton, R. (1980) Emotions, Practical Knowledge and Common Culture, in *Explaining Emotions*, ed. A. O. Rorty, Berkeley: University of California Press.

Scruton, R. (1986) *Sexual Desire*, London: Weidenfeld.

Stocker, M. (1979) Desiring the Bad: An Essay in Moral Psychology, *Journal of Philosophy*, 76.

Taylor, G. (1976) Love, *Proceedings of the Aristotelian Society*, 76.

Taylor, R. (1982) *Having Love Affairs*, Buffalo: Promethus Books.

Tov-Ruach, L. (1980) Jealousy, Attention and Loss, in *Explaining Emotions*, ed. A. O. Rorty, Berkeley: University of California Press.

Trigg, R. (1970) *Pain and Emotion*, Oxford: Clarendon.

Vendler, Z. (1967) *Linguistics in Philosophy*, Ithaca: Cornell University Press.

Index

Abraham, Karl, 22–3
Albee, Edward, 30
appeal, degree of, 112–13
Aquinas, St. Thomas, 120
Aristotle, 3, 15, 27, 94, 125
attitudes
  dispositional, 98
  and emotions, 3, 95–9
  evaluative, 99–100
  founded on beliefs, 96–7
  and universal objects, 95–7

Bedford, Errol, 5
beliefs
  attitudes founded on, 94–9
  changes of, 81–3
  and expression of attitudes, 99
  specific, about beloved, 15, 78
Boccherini, Luigi, 31

care
  disinterested, 26–9
  loving, 56–7
Casanova's Chinese Restaurant, 29
Chéri, 66
Christ, Jesus, 23
Coleridge, S.T., 77
Colette, 66–7
concepts, criteria of, 113–14, 124–5

danger, and fear, 111–12

desire
  blind, 38–9, 80
  and effects, 101
  sexual, 47–53, 60–5
De Sousa, Ronald, 3
dispositions, and occurrences, 85–6, 98, 115–17
Donne, John, 2
Douglas, Lord Alfred, 38

effects, physiological, 55–6, 100–1
Eliot, George, 72
emotions
  ambiguity of term, 9–10, 101–2
  anger, 15–16, 125
  Aristotle's definition of, 3
  and attitudes, 3
  attitudes, evaluative, 98–100
  changes, physiological, 55–6, 100–2
  characterization of, 100–1
  connected concepts, 10–11
  fear, 3–4, 89, 97, 110–12, 114–17
  fright response, in infants, 93
  hatred, 124–6
  identification of, 92–3
  indignation, 16
  judgments in, 5–10, 120–6
  liking, distinction from, 19–20
  numbers of, 14
  objects of, 94–5

131

Emotions (*cont.*)
    practical, 15
    sensations, bodily, 100
    universal and particular, 94–7
evil, 115
    doing of, 120
    inherent, 125

fairy tale, of prince and toad, 45
fear, 3–4, 89, 97
    and danger, 111–12
    in infants, 93
    and love, 114–17
feelings, momentary
    emotions, 2, 77
    expression of, 91
    misidentification of, 91–2
    sensations and physiological
        changes, 100
Fenichel, Otto, 36–7, 68, 70
Fisher, S., 50
Fontane, Theodor, *Effi Briest*, 75
Fortenbaugh, W., 16
Freud, S., 10, 37–8
friendship, 27

Goldberg, S.L., 45
Goldman, Alan, 2, 47–9, 62
Grunewald, Matthias, 31

Hamlyn, David, 1
Handel, G.F., *Saul*, 26
Harunobu, 25
hatred, 124–6
Hunter, J.M.F., 1, 50, 53, 71–2

irrationality, 118–23

judgments
    of beloved, 39–40
    in emotions, 5–9
    of intrinsic worth, 120–4

kleptomania, 37
Kubie, Lawrence, 40

Leibniz, G.W., 23
libido, in schizophrenia, 22–3
love
    being in love, 71–2
    characterization of, 45–6, 77
    decisions concerning, 84–5
    evaluations in, 111
    good will in, 29
    group bond, 10
    infatuation, kinds of, 35–6, 38–
        9, 78–9
    of means, 24–5
    of nonpersons, 20–3, 25–6, 103–
        6
    object and ego, 37–8
    object as particular, 103–4
    of persons, 25–6, 41–6, 102–10,
        117–19
    reciprocity of, 1, 28–9, 30
    as relationship, open-ended,
        106–9
    of self, 20–3
    self-interrogation in, 73–5
    strength of, 86–8
    unique relationship, 106–10, 114
    universal objects, 104–7
luck, gambling, 36–7
Lyons, William, 56, 111

Man of Honour, 52
Marx, Karl, 125
Middlemarch, 72

neurosis, in marriage, 40
Newton-Smith, W., 33

occurrences, and dispositions, 85–
    6, 97–8, 116–17

133